GHOST TOWNS OF COLORADO

Your Guide to Colorado's
Historic Mining Camps
and Ghost Towns

Text by Philip Varney
Photographs by John Drew

Voyageur Press

A Pictorial
Discovery Guide

Dedication

For Jim Janoviak and Karen Daly.

Edited by Amy Rost-Holtz
Designed by Kristy Tucker and Andrea Rud
Cover designed by Kristy Tucker
Printed in Hong Kong

First hardcover edition
99   00   01   02   03   5   4   3   2   1
First softcover edition
05   06   07   08   09   9   8   7   6   5

Library of Congress Cataloging-in-Publication Data
Varney, Philip.
   Ghost towns of Colorado : your guide to Colorado's historic mining camps and ghost towns / text by
Philip Varney ; photography by John Drew.
      p.   cm. — (A pictorial discovery guide)
   Includes bibliographical references and index.
   ISBN 0-89658-416-X. — ISBN 0-89658-418-6 (alk. paper)
   1. Colorado—Guidebooks. 2. Colorado—History, Local. 3. Ghost towns—Colorado—Guidebooks. 4. Mining
camps—Colorado—Guidebooks. 5. Colorado—Pictorial works. I. Title. II. Series.
   F774.3.V37   1999
   917.8804'33—dc21   98-37523
                                 CIP

Distributed in Canada by Raincoast Books, 8680 Cambie Street, Vancouver, B.C. V6P 6M9

Published by Voyageur Press, Inc.
123 North Second Street, P.O. Box 338, Stillwater, MN 55082 U.S.A.
651-430-2210, fax 651-430-2211
books@voyageurpress.com   www.voyageurpress.com

Educators, fundraisers, premium and gift buyers, publicists, and marketing managers: Looking for creative products and new sales ideas? Voyageur Press books are available at special discounts when purchased in quantities, and special editions can be created to your specifications. For details contact the marketing department at 800-888-9653.

Excerpt from *The Life of an Ordinary Woman* by Anne Ellis. Copyright 1929 by Anne Ellis, © renewed 1957 by Neita Carey and Earl L. Ellis. Reprinted by permission of Houghton Mifflin Co. All rights reserved.

Page 1: *Fall graces the Como Cemetery.*
Pages 2–3: *St. Elmo's main street has a genuine "ghost town" look.*
Page 3, inset: *Placer gold rests in the pan of a balance scale.*
Facing page: *A residence at Ironton sits in silence.*

CONTENTS

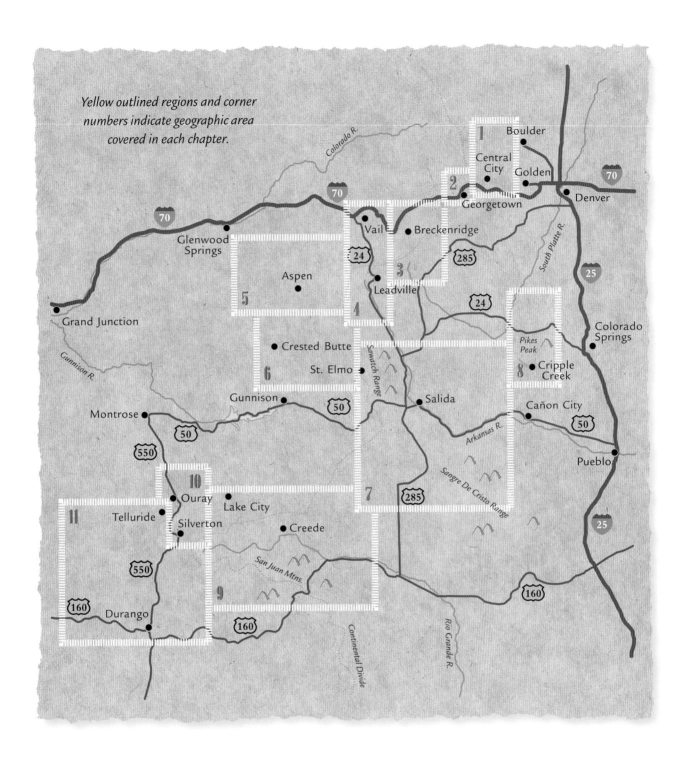

Yellow outlined regions and corner numbers indicate geographic area covered in each chapter.

TO THE READER

In the summer of 1955, I sat in the back seat of a brand-new Buick as I accompanied my best friend on his family's vacation. I was eleven at the time, and this young Illinois boy had never seen a mountain. I watched in disbelief as the plains of eastern Colorado began to display an astonishing western horizon.

We stayed for a week at a dude ranch somewhere near Idaho Springs. We took a four-wheel-drive trip to an old mine. I have never been quite the same since that trip. Although I now live in Arizona and have written mostly about the Southwest, everything I have published evolved from that vacation in Colorado.

I have been visiting Colorado regularly since the 1970s. I first saw many of the state's ghost towns while crossing its great passes on a road bike or mountain bike. If you think it is exciting to come upon an abandoned town in a four-wheel-drive vehicle, try struggling there on a bicycle.

This is my fifth book on ghost towns. The first was written as a result of my frustration with the way most ghost town books were organized. I wanted a practical, informative guide that would give me the details I needed next to me on the seat of my truck. When I eventually wrote my own book, I decided to arrange the towns geographically, so readers could visit them in logical groups.

That is how this book is arranged, as well, beginning just west of Denver with Central City, Black Hawk, and Idaho Springs—the earliest camps in the 1859 Gold Rush—and extending from there all the way to Durango, Dolores, and Rico in Colorado's southwest corner.

Each chapter has a brief overview of the area, a map, specific directions to each site, and recommendations for the type of vehicle needed. Some towns are adjacent to an interstate, while others are along back roads that require four-wheel drive. For one site, we had to leave our truck behind and hike.

Fairplay's South Park City features a nineteenth-century barber shop equipped with personalized shaving mugs, hair tonic, and cologne.

By my definition, a ghost town has two characteristics: the population has decreased markedly, and the initial reason for its settlement (such as a mine or a railroad) no longer keeps people there. A ghost town can be completely deserted, like Sneffels, Alta, or Turret; it can have a few current residents, like St. Elmo, Gold Hill, or Como; or it can have genuine signs of vitality, like Silver Plume, Marble, and Pitkin.

People in places like Victor, Creede, and Leadville may be offended about inclusion in a "ghost town" book. But even a town like Victor has ghost town indicators—its population dropped from five thousand to three hundred; a church is vacant; a school has no students; many stores are shuttered.

Although I had seen most of the towns many times, I visited or revisited every single site in 1997. The color photographs in this book were all taken between 1996 and 1998. This book's emphasis is on what remains at a site, not what was there in its heyday. I describe what to look for at each site, and, with major places such as Leadville and Silverton, I give suggestions for walking and driving tours to view some of the towns' most architecturally interesting and historic buildings.

I include information about a town's cemeteries, if it has any. Personally, I find graveyards fascinating, touching, and puzzling—often they raise questions they do not answer. Cemeteries are a tangible piece of our past that often survive when buildings do not.

Throughout the book, I also make recommendations about attractions such as museums, train rides, and mill or mine tours. To see them all would be expensive and somewhat repetitious, so when such attractions come up, I give advice based on comparisons to similar tours. Incidentally, I paid for all tours, and guides knew me only as another tourist.

I hope that this book and its photographs will entice

The Duncan residence in Animas Forks is one of Colorado's more photographed buildings.

you to visit these places for yourself. But when you go, please remember that ghost towns are fragile places. I do not collect artifacts from sites, although I have seen items that tempted me. Leave a site as you found it. If you must pick up something, how about a film wrapper or an aluminum can?

A notice posted on a wall in a lovely old house in Ironton says it perfectly:

Attention: We hope that you are enjoying looking at our heritage. The structure may last many more years for others to see and enjoy if everyone like you treads lightly and takes only memories and pictures.

The San Juan Advocates

Philip Varney
Tucson

Introduction

"PIKES PEAK OR BUST!"

For argonauts heading to California's 1849 Gold Rush, the Rocky Mountains were an obstacle to avoid or overcome. Ten years later, the Rockies became the object of their own stampede. An estimated one hundred thousand people, mostly young men, crossed the Kansas Territory's dusty plains to the foot of the Rockies in 1859. About three-quarters ultimately went home disappointed because of exaggerated accounts (Mark Twain defined a mine as "a hole in the ground owned by a liar"), but the success stories fill Colorado's history books.

Nine men (and no women) pose for posterity on their way west in search of Colorado gold. (Courtesy of the Denver Public Library, Western History Collection)

The first gold strikes were made in the spring of 1859 in the Idaho Springs and Central City areas (chapter one), followed almost immediately by silver discoveries in Georgetown and Silver Plume (chapter two). By that summer, intrepid prospectors headed farther west for bonanzas in the higher elevations around Breckenridge (chapter three).

These prospectors attracted miners, followed by merchants, saloonkeepers, clergy, lawmakers—and lawbreakers. All depended upon the mines in one way or another. Mines also needed roads to get ore to market, bringing in road builders, muleskinners, and teamsters. Toll roads ultimately gave way to railroads, resulting in higher profits for mines as lower-grade ores could be transported more economically.

In the early 1870s, the great southwestern mines boomed in the San Juan Mountains (chapters nine, ten, and eleven). In 1876, Colorado achieved statehood, an event accelerated considerably by its mineral wealth. Incredible silver deposits were found in 1878 at Leadville (chapter four), and in 1880 at Aspen (chapter five).

Gold and silver are more valuable, but coal is essential to railroads and to any large-scale mining operation, so deposits found in the early 1880s at Crested Butte (chapter six) and near Redstone (chapter five) became significant bonanzas of their own. At about the same time, more silver and gold strikes around St. Elmo and Silver Cliff (chapter seven) sent prospectors scurrying to those areas.

The last great silver bonanza occurred in Creede (chapter nine). It was the last because the repeal of the Sherman Silver Purchase Act in 1893 changed the rules. At that time, the federal government stopped purchasing a set amount of silver and returned to the Gold Standard. The result was a silver crash that sent places such as Georgetown, Leadville, Aspen, Silverton, Lake City, and Creede into tailspins. But the discovery of fabulous gold deposits in the early 1890s at Cripple Creek and Victor (chapter eight) brought thousands of unemployed silver miners to the towns near Battle Mountain.

Mining towns are created to fail, as they exist to extract a finite quantity of ore, and when that quantity is gone, the town is doomed, unless it can find another way to prosper. Pinched-out ore bodies, labor disputes, World War I, and the Great Depression all contributed to the decline of Colorado mining.

When other states profited from the great production effort of World War II, Colorado's mines actually suffered because of Gold Limitation Order L-280, which essentially closed mines that were not producing strategic materials. But one seemingly minor World War II event significantly improved the state's long-range economic outlook. Camp Hale, a training facility for skiing mountain troops, used the slopes at Aspen and ushered in the ski resort. Skiing proved to be a new bonanza, a kind of gold supply that doesn't seem to run out for the once-moribund mining towns of Aspen, Breckenridge, Crested Butte, and Telluride. The summer tourist trade has also brought prosperity to those ski towns, as well as to places like Durango, Silverton, Lake City, and Frisco.

Other towns have found prosperous post-mining lives in limited-stakes gambling. Since 1991, the industry has created a two-edged sword for Black Hawk, Central City, and Cripple Creek. Gambling dollars have revitalized the communities and helped with preservation efforts for historic buildings, but huge casinos have so altered the face of those colorful towns that a Denver cartoonist, in a strip showing a string of glitzy behemoths, asked, "Did they have to kill Black Hawk to save it?"

To experience Colorado's mining history, one can explore its remnants: the ghost towns and mining camps that were left behind when the riches faded. Most have vanished completely. Others have a reminder or two to prove they existed. A few have significant structures and mining evidence. A handful of towns thrive, even though their mines have since closed. This book contains eighty-eight sites; an additional sixty were visited but not included either because little of historic significance remains or the public is prohibited from visiting the site.

Why are so many people fascinated with ghost towns? Mystery writer Tony Hillerman, in a foreword to my New Mexico book, put it perfectly: "To me, to many of my friends, to scores of thousands of Americans, these ghost towns offer a sort of touching-place with the past. We stand in their dust and try to project our imagination backward into what they were long ago. Now and then, if the mood and the light and the weather are exactly right, we almost succeed."

Our "touching-places with the past" are to be explored and photographed, but also protected and treasured. Please be a part of the preservation, not the destruction.

Ward's two-story Columbia Hotel is unusual because its back wall is not parallel to its front. The rear of the building is built on an angle to conform to a hill behind it.

Chapter One

CENTRAL CITY GHOSTS

Left: *Russell Gulch has several standing ruins that demonstrate the skill of the Cornish stonemasons who erected them.*

Above: *A doorknob and lockset block entry to a weathered building in Gold Hill.*

Gold fever! This is the area where the Colorado Gold Rush began, the "Pikes Peak or Bust" frenzy that brought one hundred thousand people to Colorado in 1859 alone. The three earliest mining camps created during that population explosion are discussed in this chapter: Idaho Springs, where the first placer deposits were found; Gold Hill, site of early placer and later primary deposits; and Central City, where the first and richest lode gold was discovered.

The sites described in this chapter vary today from casino meccas, such as Central City and Black Hawk, to almost deserted ghosts, such as Apex and Wallstreet. In between is the charm of Idaho Springs and the somnolence of Nevadaville, Russell Gulch, and Gold Hill. To make exploring easy, all sites are located within a short drive from downtown Denver and all can be reached by passenger car.

Central City and Black Hawk

Central City and Black Hawk have been rivals since 1859, and proponents of either might object to my combining them as one entry. But their history and geography are so interconnected that it is almost impossible to write about one without including the other.

Central City and Black Hawk are bustling gambling towns now. Not too long ago, both were nearly ghost towns. When they were key players in the gold fever, they were bursting with life.

In January 1859, placer gold discoveries were made along Clear Creek (see Idaho Springs entry). On May 6 of that year, Georgian John H. Gregory staked a claim that established the first gold lode in Colorado. The excitement along Clear Creek turned into a mad rush in Gregory Gulch. Several thousand prospectors were at work in less than a month. Within two months, thirty thousand people were fueling the gold frenzy in the gulch that had been called "The Richest Square Mile on Earth."

The camp that formed was Gregory Diggings, later called Mountain City. A post office was established in that name in January 1860, but the town was simply absorbed by Central City, its neighbor to the west. Central City was likely named because it was central among area mining camps. Black Hawk was a secondary part of the gold rush. Located down the gulch from

Black Hawk became known as "The City of Mills." This 1879 photograph shows the Bobtail Mill with Black Hawk spreading down the canyon beyond. (Photo by Charles Weitfle. Courtesy of the Ted Kierscey Photo Collection.)

Gregory Diggings, it was probably named because a mill erected there came from the Black Hawk Company of Rock Island, Illinois. While water was scarce to its upper-gulch neighbors, Black Hawk had an abundant supply, located as it was along the North Branch of Clear Creek. Because it had the enormous quantities of water necessary to power several mills, Black Hawk became known as the "City of Mills."

When early surface gold and easily retrieved primary deposits along Gregory Gulch were depleted, miners found that remaining hard-rock veins contained complex sulfide ores. The initial mining boom was over.

In 1867, however, Nathaniel Hill, a Brown University professor, put his theories of extracting gold from sulfide ore into practice by erecting in Black Hawk the first successful smelter in the territory, the Boston and Colorado Smelting Works. This smelter solidified Black Hawk's importance in a rebounding mining industry. Ore could now be shipped in concentrate, significantly lowering transportation costs.

The result was another boost in the economies of both

Gold miners often looked for quartz outcroppings in trying to find primary gold deposits. This native gold on quartz shows why.

14

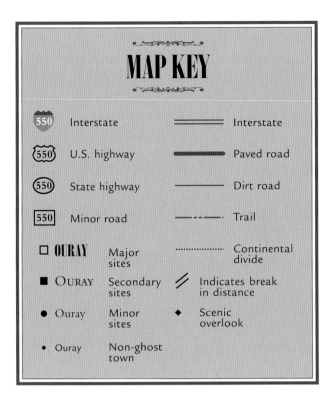

MAP KEY

🛡550	Interstate	═══════	Interstate
🛡550	U.S. highway	▬▬▬▬▬	Paved road
🛡550	State highway	─────	Dirt road
550	Minor road	─ ─ ─ ─	Trail
□ **OURAY**	Major sites	··············	Continental divide
■ **OURAY**	Secondary sites	⫽	Indicates break in distance
● Ouray	Minor sites	◆	Scenic overlook
∙ Ouray	Non-ghost town		

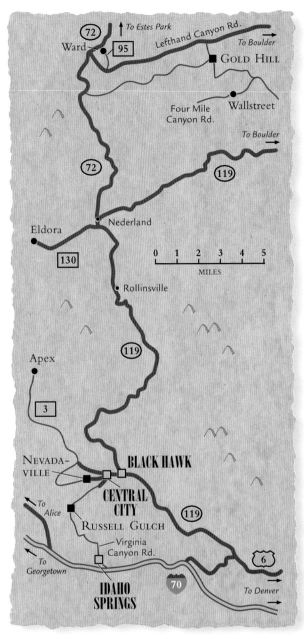

cities. Black Hawk was relegated, however, to blue collar status, while Central City became a grand lady of the Rockies, with a luxury hotel and an opulent opera house. While Black Hawk could claim Colorado's first permanent school, Central City residents could sneer that although theirs was second, it was made of stone, not merely wood frame.

The best ore bodies near Central City were depleted by the 1880s; from then until the early 1900s, area mines were still steady producers, but the bonanza times were over. Mining continued as shafts went deeper, but inflation and the unchanging price of gold made mining less profitable. Before and after World War I, buildings in both towns were dismantled and moved to other communities. Although mining continued on a lesser scale, Central City and Black Hawk seemed headed toward obscurity.

Tourism brought the area somewhat back to life beginning in the 1950s, when I first gaped at the towns as a wide-eyed eleven-year-old. They were then dying, but not dead, as curious visitors glimpsed a past that was colorful but, for the townspeople, not particularly profitable.

When casino gambling came to Central City and Black Hawk in 1991, the stakes literally changed, for better or worse. Today the "Richest Square Mile on Earth" doesn't try to remove pockets of gold from the hills; it tries to remove some of the gold from your pockets. You have to sift through the casinos' glitz and the slot machines' constant jingle to find authentic elements of Black Hawk and Central City. But if you make the effort, you will find, well, a jackpot of history.

Walking and Driving Around Black Hawk

Most visitors enter Black Hawk first, so here are a few places to see there.

The town's most famous residence, the Lace House, will not be where I last saw it, because it is to be relocated to somewhere within Black Hawk. Built in 1863, the Lace House features extensive jigsaw-created wooden gingerbread. Although not Colorado's grandest residence, the Lace House has a delicacy and grace that make it justifiably revered. Inquire as to its present location.

15

Above: *Central City's seven cemeteries offer an amazing variety of markers. These forlorn headstones rest in the I. O. O. F. Cemetery.*

Left: *Black Hawk's Lace House shows off its jigsaw gingerbread. According to architect and author C. Eric Stoehr, it is "the purest and most elaborately detailed remaining example of the Carpenter Gothic."*

Two historic buildings that should stay put (they are on a hill strategically removed from casino real estate) are the 1863 Presbyterian church and the 1870 Black Hawk Schoolhouse, located on the north side of Gregory Gulch on Church Street. The church, whose bell was brought across the prairie by ox cart, was donated to the adjacent school in 1907 to be used as a gymnasium. It currently is the city hall annex. The schoolhouse served its original purpose until 1960, stood vacant for more than thirty years, and then became the police station.

The main city hall, erected in 1877, is immediately below the church and school in the central business district. Originally the fire department used the first floor, with city offices on the second.

The cemetery is 5.6 miles from town. Take State Route 119 north from downtown Black Hawk for 5.1 miles and turn right on Golden Gate Canyon Road (State Route 46). Then take the first right, which is Dory Canyon Road. The cemetery is located on the east side of the road, opposite the large, modern county building.

Above: *The Central City Opera House, which is still in use, is known for its excellent acoustics.*

Below: *The Opera House (right foreground) and Teller House hotel (beyond the opera house) are the most elegant buildings in splendid Central City.*

Between Black Hawk and Central City

To visit the place where it all began, stop at the historical monument on the south side of the road .4 of a mile west of downtown Black Hawk and .6 of a mile east of Central City.

The monument's plaque commemorates where John Gregory found gold in 1859. Across the street are remnants of his diggings.

Walking and Driving Around Central City

A good place to begin your tour of Central City is the Schoolhouse Museum, located on High Street, one block north of the highway. There you will find displays and memorabilia provided by the Gilpin County Historical Society. Downtown Central City features many buildings from the gold rush days. Two structures of particular interest are the Teller House and the Central City Opera House, both located on Eureka Street. Tours of the buildings begin on the hour at the Teller House. The 1872 Teller House was considered one of the West's finest hotels. When President Ulysses S. Grant visited in 1873, silver bricks worth sixteen thousand dollars were placed so

he would have a path appropriate for a president as he walked from his carriage to the Teller House. Because gold made Central City famous, he is supposed to have inquired why they had chosen silver. The answer? Gold was too common.

The 750-seat opera house was constructed in 1878 by Cornish stonemasons and features a central chandelier, hickory chairs, and decorative murals.

Beyond the opera house at 209 Eureka Street is the 1874 Thomas-Billings House, which was a wedding present in the early 1890s to Marcia Billings and her husband Ben Thomas from her parents. The house's furnishings are virtually complete, with more than four thousand items belonging to the Thomases.

Eureka Street continues northwest for a mile from Central City to six of its seven cemeteries. The cemeteries fan out around a triangle intersection of roads. Starting across from the Boodle Mill, the graveyard farthest to the northwest is the I. O. O. F. Cemetery. One headstone there consists of an unusual log cabin for William R. Walter, who died in 1899 at twenty-one years of age. Another

An unusual tin-encased headframe stands beyond stone ruins in Nevadaville. The headframe is south of the road that leads to the Bald Mountain Cemetery.

marker is for Sarah Stevens. She was born in 1796, the earliest birth date I can recall on a Colorado headstone. She died in 1872.

East of the I. O. O. F. is a small cemetery for the Red Man Lodge. Behind it is the large Catholic Cemetery, where many natives of Italy, Ireland, and Germany are buried. The most interesting feature here is a double-thick, brick beehive, ovenlike structure. According to author Alan Granruth, its purpose is a mystery. He thinks perhaps it served as a temporary burial location during winter months when digging a grave would have been difficult. It is also conceivable that it simply predates the cemetery and was a kiln to convert wood to charcoal.

The Knights of Pythias Cemetery is across the road to the east. Adjacent to it is the City of Central Cemetery. Most older graves are found in the southeast corner. Beyond that cemetery is a small graveyard for the Ancient Order of the Foresters.

Central City's Masonic Cemetery is on the other side of town. Information about it is included in the next entry, Nevadaville.

When You Go

Black Hawk is 33 miles west of Denver. Take I-70 west to exit 244 and follow the signs to Black Hawk. Central City is a mile west of Black Hawk.

Nevadaville

Nevadaville is a genuine ghost town. Because it is perched near parking lots of its larger neighbor, one can only hope progress will ignore it, and Central City will not swallow it up.

Nevadaville came to life with the Gregory Diggings excitement of 1859 as miners clambered around every hill and gulch in the area. Citizens of the new community called it Nevada City (probably in hopeful emulation of the successful gold town in California). The post office was originally granted in 1861 as Nevada, but eight years later the postal service switched the name to Bald Mountain (for a prominent peak west of town). Although citizens largely ignored the new name, eventually preferring Nevadaville, the post office stubbornly hung on as Bald Mountain until it closed in 1921.

During its heyday, as many as six thousand people lived in Nevadaville, many of them Cornish or Italian. Each group had its own neighborhood on either end of town, but they met in the thirteen downtown saloons for occasional donnybrooks. The two groups later united against a common enemy—Chinese laborers willing to accept lower wages.

High above Nevadaville on the northeast end of town is the Prize Mill. The missing floorboards, broken glass, and exposed nails make the mill, like most ghost town buildings, a dangerous place to explore.

Water was constantly in short supply, at one time selling for a steep forty cents a barrel. A water company that furnished Nevadaville was once accused of diverting its supplies to a preferred customer, Central City. The boom days were the 1860s and 1870s, but Nevadaville had recurring periods of modest prosperity in the late 1890s, before World War I, and into the 1930s.

Today, Nevadaville has several surviving historic buildings. If you are coming from Central City, the first you will see is a strange stone structure on your left. This building reportedly once served Chinese residents as a Buddhist temple. Just .1 of a mile before it, on the opposite side of the street, is the road to Central City's Masonic Cemetery. There I found two graves that were quite touching, for they reflected something I had never seen before. Thomas and Elizabeth Warren buried their daughter Minnie in 1876 after fourteen months of life. They named their next daughter Minnie as well, and she died in 1877 at only eight months.

In Nevadaville's main business district you will find the Bald Mountain Trading Post and the 1879 Masonic Block. Across the street stand a brick and stone falsefront store, the wood-frame combination city hall and fire department, and another brick store. Extensive mining debris spreads along Nevada Gulch below town.

Nevadaville's graveyard is the Bald Mountain Cemetery. One marker testifies to the perils of mining: "In affectionate remembrance of Andrew Martin, died June 2, 1888, age thirty-four, from injuries received at the Etna Mine." To reach this cemetery, drive west from Nevadaville on Road 273 for 1.2 miles, then turn left onto Road 2732 and follow it .2 of a mile. Road 273, incidentally, continues to the main Central City cemeteries.

When You Go
Nevadaville is 2 miles southwest of Central City on Nevada Street.

Russell Gulch

William Green Russell came to Colorado with his two brothers as a veteran argonaut, having worked the Georgia and California gold fields. His first Colorado discoveries, although meager, were made in 1858 at the confluence of the South Platte River and Cherry Creek, near what is now downtown Denver.

Russell and another Georgian, John Gregory, knew that placer gold on the plains likely meant primary deposits in the mountains and so headed into the Rockies as soon as weather permitted in the spring of 1859.

The camp of Russell Gulch grew from the discoveries Russell found four miles southwest of Gregory's Diggings. That Fourth of July, miners in the gulch stopped work and assembled for a celebration. They opened the program by shooting their revolvers, once for their country, once for Pikes Peak, once for Russell, and once for John Gregory. They then listened to a speech and hoisted a homemade Old Glory created from denim overalls, a white shirt, and red longjohns. A banquet followed, consisting of bean soup, trout, antelope, biscuits, dried apples, and coffee "in tin cups, to be washed clean for the occasion."

The miners had good reason to celebrate. Only four months after they located free gold, Russell Gulch was producing an average of thirty-five thousand dollars per week for the eight hundred miners who had assembled there. That fall they formed the Russell District, which included a rather liberal law for the time: "Discovery Claims—Females have the same right as males."

The placer deposits eventually gave out, but lode mining continued into the 1880s before the town declined. During Prohibition the mines came alive again, this time as hideouts for stills.

A Russell Gulch ore car waits for a payload that will never come from a small headframe. Behind stands the sturdy brick school.

Along Russell Gulch Road today, huge walls erected by skilled Cornish stonemasons will be on your left, followed by nicely maintained homes across the gulch, more stone foundations, and the attractions of downtown Russell Gulch. The best buildings are the 1895 Odd Fellows Hall, a two-story stone building with an attractive brick facade, and the two-story brick school behind and to the east of it.

To visit the cemetery, head south on Virginia Canyon Road on the west end of town for .1 of a mile and turn west. Take the middle road where there are three forks. In .3 of a mile from Virginia Canyon Road, turn left to the cemetery.

When You Go
Russell Gulch is 2.3 miles southwest of Central City. Take Virginia Canyon Road, which eventually goes to Idaho Springs. On the way to Russell Gulch you will pass through the Glory Hill Gold Mine. Russell Gulch Road heads off to the left .2 of a mile after that mine. Follow this road into the townsite.

Idaho Springs

Idaho Springs was one of Colorado's original mining camps, and original it remains. It has not been over-

This combination headframe and bin near the Stanley Mines complex can be viewed from Interstate 70 as you drive a half mile west from Idaho Springs.

meaning "gem of the mountain" or "light on the mountain," but the author of *Idaho Place Names* categorically states that it is a coined word with no Indian origin.)

Within a few months of its founding, Idaho Springs boasted 150 homes, 10 saloons, various businesses, and a hotel.

Placer deposits gave out, but primary lodes discovered in the canyons above town in the mid-1860s assured the town's longevity. For six years Idaho Springs held the county seat as hastily constructed frame buildings were replaced by brick edifices. In the 1870s the purported medicinal properties of the hot springs attracted health seekers, and the waters were also bottled for shipment nationwide. A narrow gauge railroad was extended to Idaho Springs, making it easier for tourists to test the waters and for mining companies to ship their ore.

In 1892, construction began on two drainage and haulage tunnels. The larger, the Newhouse (later called the Argo) Tunnel, extended 4.2 miles to Central City and took seventeen years to complete. It did its job, draining several old mines, opening rich veins, and providing cheap ore transportation.

The Argo Mill was erected near the tunnel's mouth. It operated from 1913 until 1943, when a dynamite blast released a deluge of water that killed four miners and closed the tunnel, effectively ending large-scale mining and milling in Idaho Springs.

Walking and Driving Around Idaho Springs

Begin your visit to Idaho Springs at the visitor information center, located immediately west of where Miner Street splits from Colorado Boulevard. Along with picking up a walking tour map, be sure to examine the displays, including a handsome ladder wagon from 1878. That was the year Idaho Springs established a fire department—but only after a brewery burned.

Downtown Idaho Springs is best covered on foot. Starting on the east end at Seventeenth and Miner, you will see the attractive city hall, formerly the Grass Valley School, which was relocated in 1986.

Behind city hall are an 1886 Colorado and Southern narrow-gauge locomotive, tender, and passenger car. A short walk from there is lovely Bridal Veil Falls and the huge Charley Tayler water wheel, which Tayler fashioned in 1893 to power a stamp mill on Ute Creek. A sign there mentions that Tayler bragged that his good health was due to the fact that he had never bathed or kissed a woman. It seems like a classic case of cause and effect.

Most buildings along Miner Street have informative plaques, so their history can be left to your reading. Consider visiting the Underhill Museum, located in the of-

whelmed by casinos like Black Hawk, nor has it been made chic by ski resorts like Aspen. Idaho Springs is a delightful place to explore.

George A. Jackson was an experienced prospector, having spent four years in the California Gold Rush. In January 1859, despite severe cold weather, he ventured into the Rockies with several companions. Eventually heading out on his own, he discovered placer deposits at the point where Clear Creek was joined by another. In order to do any panning, he had to build fires to thaw the ground and melt snow to wash for gold. But he knew what he had found, so he marked the spot and left the mountains to wait for better weather.

Jackson met a group of Chicagoans who joined him in organizing the Chicago Mining Company. When the group returned to the spot where Jackson had made his find, they dubbed the second stream Chicago Creek and panned nineteen hundred dollars in gold in a week. When Jackson returned to the Denver area and purchased supplies with gold dust, the rush was on.

The camp that grew near the discovery was called first called Jackson's Diggings, then Sacramento Flats, Sacramento City, Idahoe City, Idaho, and finally Idaho Springs. The "springs" was added because of nearby hot springs. ("Idaho" has been variously described as an Indian word fice of assayer James Underhill and operated by the Historical Society of Idaho Springs, which offers displays and memorabilia of local interest.

The main historic district ends at Fourteenth Street, but go just beyond to see the 1904 Carnegie Library (one of Colorado's few historic libraries) and the 1878 Idaho Springs Fire Department Central Hose House. The fire house is a frame building covered with pressed tin, and it has a hose drying tower behind it. Inside the firehouse is a Model AA Ford fire truck.

An enjoyable side excursion is one block east of downtown. Go south from Miner Street .2 of a mile on Soda Springs Road to Indian Springs Resort, a still-operating hot springs. The central section of the building was constructed in 1896; the wings, with their unusual dormer windows, were added in 1915.

To see several historic residences, drive Colorado Boulevard. Many homes date from the late 1880s to the early 1900s and are located between the 800 and the 1200 blocks. Four of the very nicest, with their dates of construction in parentheses, are located at 1022 (1887), 1122 (1900), 1204 (1897), and 1244 (1903).

The Idaho Springs Cemetery is located a half-mile south of town on State Route 103. On the way, turn right into the parking lot of the Clear Creek Secondary School to see a monument placed there in 1909. The historic, but distinctly unattractive, boulder on a concrete pedestal commemorates George Jackson's initial discovery of gold in the Rocky Mountains at this spot on January 7, 1859.

When you return to the highway, continue to the cemetery. You can drive almost the entirety of it, but watch

Argo Mill and Phoenix Mine Tours

Throughout this book, I comment on attractions such as trains and mill or mine tours to help you decide whether or not to make the expenditure.

It is hard to overlook the Argo Mill, because it dominates the east end of town. Despite the mill's being the biggest structure in town, I cannot say it was the best, at least when I toured it in 1997. The mill was lacking essential ingredients that cannot be replaced—the ball mill room has no ball mill, the stamp mill no stamps.

There was no one leading the tour, and explanations on the self-guiding sheet, although helpful, do not replace a well-informed guide. The display cases at the end of the tour were unclean, and unidentified photos were peeling out of frames. Frequently the glass covering the photos was broken or cracked. The yard was filled with mining equipment, but most of the items were unidentified. The Argo Mill did not measure up to the excellent Mayflower Mill Tour near Silverton (see chapter ten).

Although less elaborate and less polished than mine tours near Cripple Creek, Silverton, and Ouray, the Phoenix Mine is nevertheless an interesting tour and a good value. The tour lasts about forty minutes—shorter than some tours, which could be an advantage if you have small children. Our guide was knowledgeable, personable, and responsive to questions.

There is no mine train or descending cage to enter the mine—enticements in other tours—but the

walk we took through the tunnels was enjoyable nonetheless.

To reach the Phoenix Mine, take Stanley Road, at the west end of Idaho Springs, for 1.2 miles to Trail Creek Road. On the way you can see the buildings of the Stanley Mine. Follow Trail Creek Road for .8 of a mile to the mine.

Like virtually all mills, the Argo used gravity to aid the milling process. Buildings step down the hillside to take ore through various stages of separation from the worthless material that surrounds it.

The hotel at Apex likely was constructed in stages. The first floor is made of hewn logs, while the second floor is of lumber. The lumber false front has a decorative touch—rows of shingles below the cornice.

for muddy, slippery sections. I found two interesting stones on the upper road. One is a lovely clamshell marker for Daisy Mae Carter, who died at the age of five years in 1902. Another is a sandcast log cabin headstone, similar to one in Central City's I. O. O. F. Cemetery, for Blanche Dunton, who died at age six in 1899.

When You Go
Idaho Springs is 6.2 miles beyond Russell Gulch on Virginia Canyon Road (also known by the unsettling nickname of "Oh My God Road," but which is now quite tame and extraordinarily scenic). By paved road, Idaho Springs is 14 miles from Black Hawk and 29 miles west of Denver on I-70.

Apex

Apex is a pleasant ghost town not far from Central City. It features almost twenty rustic structures that stand in marked contrast to the elegance of Central City.

Apex developed in 1896 as the center of the Pine Creek Mining District. (Pine Creek parallels the road into town.) Soon the community had a newspaper, telephone service, and eight hundred residents.

A principal Apex mine, the Mackey, was discovered in the 1870s by Dick Mackey, but not until years later did it become a big payer—almost by accident. A man named Mountz leased the Mackey with a partner, who absconded with thirty thousand dollars of the returns on the first ore, leaving Mountz almost penniless. Mountz toiled on, carefully using his last dollars as he tunneled 110 feet trying to find the main vein. He became so discouraged that he walked into the tunnel, deposited all his dynamite, lit the fuse, and walked out. He didn't even look back at the tremendous explosion.

The next day he returned, rather indifferently surveying the result of his recklessness. He found high-grade ore in such quantities that he sprinted to his cabin and telephoned a Denver supply house, ordering a thousand ore sacks. He yelled, "I haven't a dollar, but I've struck it rich. Send the sacks on the next train." The mine became a solid producer, and the stolen thirty thousand dollars turned out to be just a fraction of the mine's value.

As you enter Apex today, you will see several hewn-log cabins on your left and concrete foundations on your right, with cabins in the trees near the road heading west. A well-constructed frame building looks as if it might have been a store or town hall. Four more hewn-log structures are followed by a two-story hotel. Beyond is a nicely preserved church or school with two more cabins farther up the road.

When You Go

Apex is 6.6 miles northwest of Central City. Take Eureka Street north to the Central City cemeteries. At the junction of roads at the cemeteries, take Road 3 north. Apex is 5.5 miles from there.

The immense ruins of the Gold Extraction Mill at Wallstreet resemble a medieval fortress.

Wallstreet

Originally called Sugar Loaf and later Delphi, Wall Street (eventually shortened to Wallstreet) earned its name because, according to the *Mining Investor* in April 1898, it was "attracting considerable attention in a large amount of capital from New York and other Eastern cities."

The Easterner who changed the name was mining promoter Charles W. Caryl, who arrived with idealistic plans. This mining camp would be different from others. Miners would have utopian conditions, including a sliding daily pay scale from two dollars up to twenty-five dollars. Utopian plans usually fail, and so did this one. In fact, idealist Caryl was eventually arrested for the very down-to-earth crime of sending obscene material through the mail.

Caryl's Gold Extraction Mining and Supply Company did, however, build a huge mill. Completed in 1902, it processed ore from several successful mines, including the Nancy, Grand View, Lion's Roost, and Gold Eagle.

The peak year of production was 1903, but after that only low-grade ore remained. The mill closed in 1905 and was later dismantled. Some mines continued to produce small quantities of ore until the early 1960s.

The first interesting structure in Wallstreet is a large residence north of the road. Farther west are the enormous stone wall and ruins of the Gold Extraction Company Mill. Beyond the mill is the picturesque Wallstreet School.

When You Go

Wallstreet is 8.8 miles northwest of Boulder. Take Canyon Boulevard west from Broadway 2.8 miles to Four Mile Canyon Road. Turn north and go 4.7 miles, then turn left. The townsite is 1.3 miles west.

Gold Hill

In January 1859, six prospectors came from Boulder Canyon to what would become Gold Hill. Shortly after George Jackson's discovery along Clear Creek (see Idaho Springs), they found the second placer deposits in the territory. These placers were found in a stream appropriately christened Gold Run. Naturally, prospectors also searched for primary veins. The most important was found by three men, including David Horsfal, for whom the claim was named.

A small stamp mill, said to be the first of its kind in Colorado, was hauled to the young camp to process Horsfal ore. Gold Hill, a small mountaintop community, prospered until the ore gave out; the town was virtually deserted by 1869.

Three years later, however, a second rush began when gold combined with tellurium was discovered at the Red Cloud Mine. Tellurium had been overlooked by early miners in the frenzy to find gold. Because improved smelting methods had been developed to make tellurium ore profitable, Gold Hill was alive again, this time relocated from the mountain to its present site.

When a forest fire threatened Gold Hill in November 1894, frightened townspeople took prized possessions and secured them in mine shafts and prospect holes. One citizen even buried his piano in his front yard. Fortunately, as the conflagration approached Gold Hill, the wind subsided, snow began to fall, and relieved townspeople extinguished the flames.

Main Street in Gold Hill today has several historic buildings, including log cabins; the 1872 two-story, hewn-log Blue Bird Lodge; the Gold Hill Inn; the Gold Hill Store; a series of wood-frame residences; and the attrac-

tive 1873 two-room schoolhouse. Pine Street, one block north, features several residences and a church with a separate bell tower.

To reach the Gold Hill Cemetery, drive south .4 of a mile on Dixon Road, which begins one block south of Main.

When You Go

Gold Hill is 5.1 miles northeast of Wallstreet. From Wallstreet, return 1.3 miles east on Four Mile Canyon Road to an intersection, where the road to Gold Hill heads north. Proceed for 3.8 miles to Gold Hill.

Ward

Ward was one of Colorado's earlier mining camps, with Calvin M. Ward filing a claim for the Miser's Dream early in 1860. The following year Cy Deardorff discovered the Columbia vein, which yielded more than $5 million in gold. By 1865, Ward's population topped six hundred.

With prosperity, however, came repeated disasters. Various fires destroyed individual buildings, including two mills. The biggest fire occurred on January 24, 1900, when a blaze started by an overheated stove in the McClancy Hotel consumed forty-five buildings. The *Ward Miner* reported, "Not a store, hotel, saloon, restaurant nor a business house of any report escaped the flames. . . ." Frontier times breed frontier spirits, however, and the *Miner* spoke for the community, saying, "We're still here. Disfigured badly of course, but you can't drown the *Miner.* . . . We expect to stay in Ward."

Between two and three dozen older buildings still stand in Ward. One of the more curious is on your left as you enter town; it is the former Catholic church that was later converted into a garage (architectural sacrilege at the very least). On a hill to the southwest is the old school, which now serves as post office, library, and town hall. Across a draw north of the school is the former Congregational church.

The main business district has a general store and other buildings. When I last visited Ward, one of its better structures—the I. O. O. F. Hall—had recently collapsed. The hall's remnants had been stored in the church-garage, and there are plans to restore it.

When You Go

Ward is 10 miles north of Nederland on State Route 72. Coming from Gold Hill, drive north on Lick Skillet Road for 1.6 miles. Then head west on Lefthand Canyon Road, which will meet Road 95 and take you to Ward.

Above: *This Gold Hill cabin has touches of civility seldom found in mining camps: a picket fence, a lantern next to the front door, and decorative (but nonfunctional) log shutters.*
Facing page: *Mining remnants stand near Eldora, which is close to a popular ski area.*

Eldora

In September 1891, John H. Kemp and seven partners formed the Happy Valley Placer, a five-hundred-acre tract along Middle Boulder Creek, to prospect for placer gold. Eventually primary deposits were also found, and in the late 1890s a rush to Happy Valley was on. In the process, the area's name was changed to something more appropriate for a gold-mining town: Eldorado Camp.

When a post office opened in 1897, the Postal Service insisted upon dropping the last syllable and using Eldora to avoid confusion with Eldorado, California. In addition to the post office, Eldora featured seven grocery stores, nine saloons, and several dance halls and gambling houses.

Soon stamp mills were constructed nearby, and the town added the Gold Miner Hotel and a two-story schoolhouse. The only thing the town lacked was a cemetery.

The boom lasted one year. Only three of the many mines were still working in 1898, and when the Colorado & Northwestern Railroad arrived in 1904, even the cheaper transportation costs it offered could not make the remaining low-grade ore profitable.

Eldora today features several attractive buildings. The main road through town is Eldorado Avenue, where you will find a log cabin, a couple of false-front stores, and the Log Cabin Market. Eldora's best building, located one block north of Eldorado Avenue on Klondike, is the 1898 Gold Miner Hotel, a two-story, rough-milled log structure with a clapboard false front.

When You Go

The closest town to Eldora is Nederland, which is 16 miles west of Boulder on State Route 119 and 10 miles south of Ward on State Route 72. From "The Hub" in Nederland, drive south .6 of a mile to road 130. Do not go to the Eldora Ski Area; stay to the right and proceed into town, 1.1 miles west of the highway.

Chapter Two

GEORGETOWN GHOSTS

Left: *The Hotel de Paris epitomizes the refinement of Georgetown. With Louis Dupuy as owner and master chef, the hotel served elegant dinners on Haviland china and featured gas lights, elaborately carved, black walnut furniture, and hot and cold running water in each guest room (an almost unheard-of luxury). This photo is of one of the two first-floor "Salesmen's Rooms" in which peddlers could show their wares by day and sleep at night, using a unique 1881-patented bed that folded up to become a desk for the day's transactions.*

Above: *Dusty dinnerware and faded lace in a Georgetown window are reminders of the town's cosmopolitan past.*

Hardly a mere "mining camp," Georgetown has an elegance, a refinement, that no other town can match. Up the hill from Georgetown is Silver Plume, whose architecture may lack the finesse of its sister to the east, but whose main street really looks like what people expect from the frontier American West.

The remaining four sites discussed in this chapter are less well known, but each offers significant attractions. Dumont, Lawson, and Empire are neighbors that feature several historic buildings. The final site, Alice, is surrounded by lovely mountain scenery.

Georgetown

Brothers George and David Griffith, farmers from Kentucky, headed to the newly discovered gold fields of Colorado in 1859 only to find the best claims in the Central City and Idaho Springs areas already taken. So they prospected farther west up Clear Creek where, in June of the same year, they found placer gold. They staked a claim and established the Griffith Mining District. Their gold discovery, however, was to be the only important one in the district.

As others joined them, a camp grew and became known as George's Town for the older Griffith brother. A second community, called Elizabethtown (probably named for the Griffiths' sister), came to life south of the first camp when silver was discovered there in 1864. These were the first mines in Colorado in which silver was mined as the principal ore, not as a lesser by-product to gold.

In 1868, Georgetown and Elizabethtown consolidated as one community. In that same year, Georgetown displaced Idaho Springs as the seat of Clear Creek County in a bitter election. By 1870, the population had climbed to eight hundred, and Georgetown settled in as "Queen of the Silver Camps" (Leadville was to become the "King"; see chapter four). In that year Georgetown citizens provided a silver spike to commemorate the rail link between Denver and Cheyenne that joined Colorado to the Union Pacific Railroad, and therefore to the rest of the nation.

By 1880, the population had soared to more than 3,000. Georgetown had schools, churches, and hotels, as well as one saloon for every 150 citizens. Four independent fire companies helped Georgetown avoid a major conflagration.

In 1893, however, disaster of another variety hit Georgetown. A steady decline in silver prices, due to increased supply and decreased coinage, culminated in the repeal of the Sherman Silver Purchase Act. This act had guaranteed acquisition of almost nine million ounces of silver per month by the federal government. Its repeal meant that the coin of the realm was gold—and only gold. This was a major blow, not just to Georgetown, but to the entire state; at the time, Colorado had been producing an astonishing 58 percent of the nation's silver. Mines and mills closed, and miners departed to gold fields in Cripple Creek (see chapter eight). Georgetown went into a precipitous decline.

Not until the middle of the twentieth century did Georgetown bloom once again, this time as a mountain retreat and tourist attraction. It and Silver Plume were declared a National Historic Landmark District, and both civic groups and private individuals began in earnest to restore their lovely towns.

Walking and Driving Around Georgetown

As you enter Georgetown's historic district, turn left across Clear Creek and right on Rose Street, one of the two major residential avenues in Georgetown (Taos, one block east, is the other). Both streets have home after lovely home, whether modest or extravagant, featuring a wide variety of nineteenth-century architectural styles.

Rose Street leads to downtown, where you will want to walk. Start at the Community Center, formerly the 1868 courthouse, at Sixth Street and Argentine. There you can pick up brochures and a free walking tour map. (However, a more helpful guide on Georgetown and Silver Plume is for sale.) Historic photos are on display in the first-floor courtroom, where district court was held. The county courtroom, jury deliberation rooms, and public restrooms are upstairs.

Sixth Street contains too many fine commercial structures to enumerate here. If you go inside only one, visit the marvelous Hotel de Paris.

Frenchman Adolphe Francois Gerard immigrated to New York in 1868 at twenty-two and headed west with the U.S. Cavalry. He deserted in Cheyenne, came to Denver in 1869, and changed his name to Louis Dupuy.

In 1873, Dupuy was working as a miner in Georgetown when he was injured in a dynamite explosion. He recovered and bought a small bakery, which over the years evolved into one of the finest hotels in the West.

Louis Dupuy died in 1900 at age fifty-six. He willed the hotel to his housekeeper and friend Sophie Gally,

Kits like these were used to assay ores from Colorado mines.

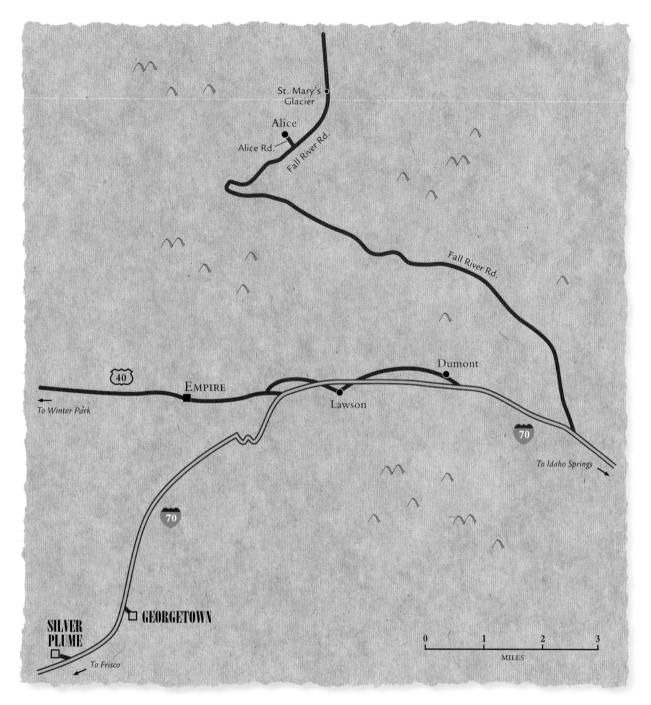

who survived him by little more than five months, dying in 1901 at sixty-six. They both are buried in the Alvarado Cemetery north of town.

The Colonial Dames of America purchased the hotel in 1954 and began a thorough restoration.

South of the main business district, on Fourth Street just east of Taos, is the 1870 Maxwell House, a private residence closed to the public. Extensively remodeled beginning in 1891, it is considered one of the country's ten best Victorian homes.

One residence open to the public and well worth touring is the opulent Hamill House, located two blocks west of the Maxwell House at 305 Argentine Street.

A fairly modest home when it was constructed in 1867, the Hamill House became a showplace when it was remodeled and expanded in 1879 by William A. Hamill, a prominent mine owner and silver speculator who had purchased the house in 1874. The elegant Gothic mansion featured a solarium, a schoolroom, and such refinements as central heating, a zinc-lined bathtub, and gold-plated doorknobs.

As mentioned earlier, Rose and Taos Streets feature many exquisite private homes. Also on Taos are the 1869 wood-frame Grace Episcopal Church; the 1918 brick Catholic church; and the lovely stone Presbyterian church, built between 1872 and 1874 (and the only Georgetown

Above: *Georgetown, once known as "Queen of the Silver Camps," has more than two hundred vintage buildings, including some of the finest in the United States.*

Right: *Touring the Hotel de Paris is a delight, from wine cellar to kitchen to dining room to spacious guest rooms such as this one, which features double beds of tiger oak and an Eastlake-style maple love seat with mahogany stain.*

church in continuous service since its construction). Across the street from the Presbyterian church is the 1874 two-story Georgetown Public School (elementary grades on the first floor, high school on the second), which proudly asserts that it is a "State of Colorado Standard School Approved Class."

Also on Taos Street, across from the city park, is the Old Missouri Firehouse, built in 1875 to protect the north end of town.

If you wish to visit Georgetown's cemetery, drive toward the interstate on-ramp, but instead of going onto I-70, proceed 3.2 miles north on Alvarado Road, which loosely parallels the highway. The Alvarado Cemetery will be on your right with a conspicuous main gate. On the other side of the road is the old Georgetown Cem-

etery, which was relocated in 1972 from the shore of Georgetown Lake.

The Alvarado Cemetery, like many large graveyards, is divided into sections for religious and fraternal groups. Hundreds of graves cover many acres, with considerable space between various sections. One of the first graves you will see is for David Griffith, the aforementioned co-founder of Georgetown, who died in 1882.

The Georgetown Loop Railroad and Lebanon Silver Mine Tour

This remarkable view of the Georgetown Loop shows four trains along the route, including one poised dramatically on Devil's High Gate Bridge. Each locomotive points to a different direction of the compass. (Photo by W. H. Jackson. Courtesy of Colorado Historical Society, negative WHJ-256)

If you plan to ride no other tourist steam train in Colorado, consider taking this one. It is more affordable than the two deservedly famous trains in southern Colorado—the Durango & Silverton and the Cumbres & Toltec—and it is much shorter, so you need not relinquish a full day. Completed in 1884, the route travels more than four and a half miles to cover the two-mile distance between Georgetown and Silver Plume, gaining 638 feet in the process. It also traverses one of the more remarkable railroad sights in the West: the 300-foot-long Devil's Gate High Bridge, where the route passes almost a hundred feet above its own tracks below.

A vintage locomotive, tender, and caboose sit near the old Georgetown station (the original Colorado & Southern depot) of the Georgetown Loop Railroad. Number 44 is a 1921 Baldwin 2-8-0 locomotive that formerly served in Central America. The caboose was number 0400 on the Rio Grande Southern line, which ran from Durango to Ridgway (see chapter eleven).

In addition, if you haven't toured a mine, consider adding the Lebanon Silver Mine Tour for a slightly increased cost. Mine tours in other parts of the state routinely cost at least twice the price of the Lebanon, but you cannot tour the mine without taking the train. Even if you decide not to ride the railroad, at least drive out to the Georgetown end to see the impressive bridge through Devil's Gate.

William Hamill added an office building (left) and a carriage house–stable (center), both made of granite cut from a Silver Plume quarry he owned, behind his magnificent home with its unusual glass conservatory (right).

The Hamill House's six-hole outhouse is Colorado's most elaborate, with a cantilevered overhang above its two entrances and a ventilating cupola. Later preservationists found pieces of expensive china, apparently broken by maids or scullions, who had dropped the pieces into the privy to conceal their clumsiness.

The dining room demonstrates the quiet elegance of Georgetown's Hamill House. The 1879 original wallpaper had to be hand painted after a 1974 fire caused smoke and water damage. The Renaissance Revival sideboard (center, rear) and the dining table are Hamill family originals.

In the Catholic section are the graves of Louis Dupuy, the celebrated owner of the Hotel de Paris, and his housekeeper Sophie Gally. The headstone features two birds looking at each other and the inscription "Deux Bon Amis" ("Two Good Friends").

To find Dupuy's and Gally's graves, go about 20 yards from the main entrance and veer to the right about 12 yards toward a wrought iron fence enclosing a grave. Beyond that, follow a road heading toward an aspen grove. In about 65 yards from the wrought iron fence, you will come to a large obelisk for William Spruance. Behind it and to the left is a bullet-shaped, terra cotta–colored marker about six and a half feet high for Dupuy and Gally.

When You Go

Georgetown is 11.6 miles west of Idaho Springs and 40 miles west of downtown Denver on I-70.

Silver Plume

As the silver claims around Georgetown flourished, late-arriving prospectors naturally tried their luck in nearby areas. The most obvious place was farther up Clear Creek, whose placer deposits had begun the strikes at both Idaho Springs and Georgetown. In the mid-1860s, another mining camp grew in a location farther up the creek as the result of that continued prospecting. In 1870, major silver discoveries there fueled a genuine bonanza.

The most colorful account of the naming of the new town involves "Commodore" Stephen Decatur, editor of Georgetown's *Colorado Miner*. He had been shown ore samples featuring feathery streaks of silver in a plume shape. When asked what to call the new but unnamed camp, Decatur proclaimed, "The name? You've already got the name! It was written on the ore you brought me!" He rhapsodized:

> The knights today are miners bold,
> Who toil in deep mines' gloom!
> To honor men who dig for gold,
> For ladies whom their arms enfold,
> We'll name the camp Silver Plume!

The rich mines were in the steep canyon walls above the new camp. They were reached by trails, many of which are still visible today, which zigzagged up from town.

One of those rich mines was the Pelican, discovered in 1868 by Owen Freeman. When he later became seriously ill and feared he was dying, Freeman confided the location to two friends. He recovered, but when he visited his claim, he learned that his "friends" had somehow neglected to include his name on the ownership papers.

Silver Plume was incorporated in 1880 and within a couple of years could claim saloons, boarding houses, butcher shops, mercantiles, fraternal lodges, a theater, a school, and Catholic and Methodist churches. With its modest frame buildings packed into narrow streets along the canyon floor, Silver Plume lacked the splendor of Georgetown. It was proudly proclaimed a "miners' town," because its more cosmopolitan neighbor was the home of mine owners and managers.

Many of those modest buildings disappeared on the night of November 4, 1884, when a fire started in Pat Barrett's saloon and spread down Main Street, consuming most of downtown. Devout women and children knelt in front of St. Patrick's Catholic Church and prayed for divine intervention. Although the fire seriously damaged the east wall, the church was spared. The next morning, Barrett's body was found in the ashes of his saloon.

Rebuilding began the next day. Citizens floated a bond issue for a water works and increased fire protection, including purchase of the town's first pumper, shipped from St. Louis. The business district was completely rebuilt by 1886, with saloons prevailing on the south side of Main Street while other businesses, such as the post office, barber shop, print shop, and mortuary, stood on the north side.

The prosperity of Silver Plume was short lived, however. Like neighboring Georgetown, the community reeled from the blow of the Silver Crash of 1893.

Walking and Driving Around Silver Plume

You enter Silver Plume from I-70 on Woodward Avenue, which features several homes and the lovely two-story 1880s New Windsor Hotel (now a private residence).

Turn left on Main Street, where you will pass the 1875 two-cell stone jail, in service until 1915. Farther west on Main is the rebuilt pump house at Brewery Springs, so named because Otto Boche's Silver Plume Brewery and Bowling Alley once stood across the street.

At Main and Hancock is the attractive Methodist church, built in the 1880s and moved to this site in 1890. It has a very austere interior except for two chandeliers, each of which features six long, elegant arms supporting a light fixture. The church is still in use; when I looked in during one visit, empty champagne bottles from a recent wedding were sitting on a table.

Still farther west is the two-story, four-classroom, 1894 brick school. A sign proclaims that this school, like the one in Georgetown, is a "State of Colorado Standard School Approved Class." Today the building is the George Rowe Museum, named for an eighty-seven-year resident of Silver Plume who donated much of the memorabilia inside.

Silver Plume's business district has more than a dozen historic buildings, including the 1886 Hose Company No.1 and Town Hall, the 1904 bandstand, the 1874 St. Patrick's Church (enlarged after the 1884 fire), and the Knights of Pythias Castle Hall. The Castle Hall was moved from Brownsville, a vanished community west of Silver Plume, in 1895.

One poignant piece of Silver Plume's history is remembered high on a cliff west of town. Englishman Heneage Griffin owned the Seven-Thirty Mine, so named because of the starting shift time, a generous hour later than most. The superintendent was Heneage's brother Clifford, about whom a tragic story was told.

Griffin's fiancée had been found dead in his room the night before their wedding, and people surmised he joined the Colorado gold rush to escape his grief. He was a reclusive person, living not in town but in a cabin at the mine, about fifteen hundred feet above Silver Plume. An accomplished violinist, he often played from sunset until dark, much to the delight of the townspeople below, who would stay outdoors to listen and applaud appreciatively at his conclusion.

On June 10, 1887, the distant audience heard his final note—followed by a gunshot. Miners ascended the steep trail to find Griffin lying in a crude, rock-hewn tomb of his own digging. A suicide note asked that he be interred there. His brother erected a monument at the spot, reading, in part, "And in Consideration of His Own Request Buried Here."

To hike to the memorial, take the trail that begins from Main and Silver Streets. The climb is a strenuous and takes about three hours round trip. If you want to catch a glimpse of the Griffin Memorial from below, take the frontage road paralleling I-70 west from town. Shortly after it goes underneath the highway, pull off the roadway and look to the north, up Brown Gulch beyond the old mine workings. Follow the falling water up to a huge outcropping on the right side of the gulch. On top stands the memorial.

Silver Plume's cemetery is hidden from view. Go under the interstate, behind the parking lot for the Georgetown Loop Railroad (where the relocated 1884 Silver Plume Depot stands), and up Mountain Street. This street has an officious "Road Closed. Local Traffic Only" sign, but the cemetery is open to the public. Turn left on Paul Street, circle a turnaround, and park by a path near an old turnstile and retaining wall.

Like many large cemeteries, this one has several sections for religious and fraternal groups. Among the interesting stones is a large monolith with the inscription

St. Patrick's Catholic Church has been standing in Silver Plume since 1874, having been spared from a city-wide fire in 1884. The condition of the wagon in the foreground suggests it may have been there almost as long as the church.

The entrance to the Burleigh Tunnel near Silver Plume looks rusty and haggard after many years of disuse.

"Sacred to the memory of Ten Italians, victims of an avalanche February 12, 1899, erected by the public." Other Italian graves are nearby, some even inscribed in Italian.

I was touched by three virtually identical graves for Stella Roberts, Olwen Roberts, and Anna Laura Roberts. None had reached four years of age. Anna Laura drowned at two years and three months. Each had different mothers and fathers. I wondered if the fathers were all brothers.

When You Go
Silver Plume is 2.2 miles west of Georgetown on I-70.

Dumont, Lawson, and Empire

Dumont
Thousands of cars on I-70 roar past Dumont each day, and I'll bet most people barely glance at the tiny town. They are missing something.

Dumont was not a mining town but a milling and smelting site, originally settled in 1859 and called Mill City. A post office was established in 1861. The town's showplace structure was the Mill City House, constructed in 1868, which featured hand-blocked wallpaper sent from Illinois and a billiard table from New York. It served as a stage stop, opera house, and town meeting hall. One of its patrons was General Ulysses S. Grant, who stopped there

when traveling the Clear Creek Toll Road.

The town prospered only as long as nearby mines did, and by the 1870s its boom days were over. In 1880, Colonel John M. Dumont, part owner of three nearby mines, changed the name of the town to his own and attempted in vain to revive the community. An effort a decade later to establish Dumont as a gambling mecca also failed.

In Dumont today, at the stop sign as you enter the town, you will see that hewn-log Mill City House that hosted General Grant next door to the fire department. Looking across the interstate from there, you can see an old railroad depot, no longer trackside. Some other older residences stand along Mill Creek Road going north from town.

The premier building in Dumont is the 1909 school, one of the more attractive in Colorado. To see it, turn north onto the dirt road east of some storage units and follow the road as it parallels the frontage road. The schoolhouse is a one-classroom brick building with an attractive bell tower. Over the door is a sign dutifully naming it a "State of Colorado Standard School Probationary Class." Apparently it never achieved the lofty rank of "Approved," as the Georgetown and Silver Plume schools did. Behind the school is an outhouse meant to last: a two-stall, four-holer made of brick. Nearby is a well-preserved log cabin likely moved from another site.

The turnoff north to the Dumont Cemetery is west of the school. The cemetery is larger than it first appears, as graves are spread out to the east. Many older graves are in the farthest section from the gate.

Lawson
From Dumont, stay on the north frontage road and go west past the modern truck stop at Downieville and on into Lawson, 2.2 miles from Dumont.

Lawson originally depended upon the travel trade. According to Aaron Frost's 1880 history of Clear Creek County, the town was founded in the early 1870s by Alexander Lawson, owner of the Six-Mile House (six miles from Georgetown), "which was well patronized by the numerous teamsters that plied a lively and profitable business before the advent of the railroad." One wonders how Lawson's success sat with his competitor up the road in Downieville. Lawson not only established his own inn about a mile away, but he also eloped with the innkeeper's daughter.

In 1876, ore-bearing quartz was discovered on Red Elephant Mountain, and a town grew around Lawson's inn. As the mines began to fail about twenty years later, however, people vacated the town.

When Interstate 70 was constructed in the mid-1960s,

many of the best buildings in Lawson were destroyed, so today only three structures worth noting still stand. The first, as you enter town from the east, is a stone residence south of the old highway. Across the street is the 1878 schoolhouse, now a private home. At the west end of town is a boarded-up, wood-frame, false-front store proclaiming the town's name.

Empire

From Lawson, continue west on the frontage road, which goes directly into U.S. 40 near I-70. Empire is one mile west on U.S. 40.

During the winter of 1860–1861, several New York prospectors, including founding father Henry DeWitt Clinton Cowles, renamed a fledgling mining camp known as Valley City for their native Empire State. Empire City's post office opened in June 1861, and the population grew to several hundred. Only a few years later, however, the boom was over and the community was nearly deserted. Perhaps because the town had lost aspirations of being a city, the post office's name was shortened to Empire in 1886. Subsequent ore discoveries modestly improved the town's fortunes—the population in 1890 was 134; by 1900 it had increased to 276.

Empire today has about fifty historic buildings. The first stop should be the visitors' center on the east side of town. An 1860s hand-hewn log schoolhouse, the first in Clear Creek County, stands next door.

Directly west of the visitors' center is the 1898 town hall, an unusual combination of a first-floor commercial business and second-floor municipal offices. Above the stairs to the second floor hangs a barrel used to dry fire hoses. Near that barrel is a genuinely original feature: a chimney originating from the second floor.

"Tours of Empire," a handy and inexpensive booklet available at the town hall, tells about several more buildings, including the 1864 Avery House west of Main Street on Park (U.S. 40 in town). The post office once stood next door, handy for Gib Avery, an early Empire postmaster.

The most splendid building in town is the Peck House, one block north of Park on Sunny Avenue. James Peck arrived in about 1862 and became known as the "Emperor of Empire" as a result of his Atlantic Gold Mine. The original Peck House, begun in 1862, was a simple fifteen by thirty-foot frame structure. Subsequent additions in 1872 and 1880 brought hotel accommodations to the Peck's home. Although the Pecks sold the property in 1945, rumors persist that one Peck remained behind. The spirit of fourteen-year-old Gracie, who died in

Empire's Peck House expanded from a simple frame home to a hotel. It is on the National Register of Historic Places, and a sign near the door says it is the oldest hotel extant in Colorado.

1885 of tuberculosis, supposedly roams her old home.

The city cemetery stands south of town. Drive south on Main Street, heading for the city park. Turn left immediately before the park and drive east as far as you can. Here you will find several interesting markers, including one for postmaster Avery and another for Peter Geary, "Shot by G.V. Hunter, September 20, 1864, aged 35 years." A large monument on a hill honors three Empire pioneers, including Henry Cowles, founding father and "trailblazer, prospector, and judge of the miners' court."

A satellite community of North Empire, where most mines were located, was two miles north of town. If significant buildings remain, you can't see them beyond posted "no trespassing" signs.

When You Go

Dumont is 4.2 miles west of Idaho Springs and 8 miles northeast of Georgetown on I-70. Lawson is 2.2 miles west of Dumont. Empire is 2 miles west of Lawson.

Alice

The principal reason you should drive Fall River Road is to see glorious St. Mary's Glacier, but while on the road, be sure to visit Alice.

Prospectors combing the valleys above Idaho Springs were bound to pan along Fall River and Silver Creek, and in the 1860s a camp of about three hundred formed around placer deposits in a place dubbed Yorktown. When the Alice Mine was opened in 1868, the town took its name. Despite placer gold and subsequent hydraulic efforts, the initial Alice operation lasted only six months.

In August of 1881, Alice consisted of a mere fifteen or twenty tents, but in the fall the town saw a minor boom. Cabins were being built, the road to Idaho Springs was

Most of Alice's historic buildings are log cabins, many of them mere ruins.

improved, and a second ditch was constructed to bring in water for increased hydraulic operations. These operations continued on a moderate but steady basis until 1915. The American Smelting and Refining Company (ASARCO) bought the property in 1936, but operations were minimal. Alice's modest life was in decline.

As you enter town on Alice Road today, you will see an deteriorating log cabin on the right built in a kind of "duplex" fashion. That building, according to author-historian Caroline Bancroft, was the home of postmaster E. J. Harper and his wife. He conducted postal business in one half of their cabin, and Mrs. Harper served meals in the other. Bancroft ought to know. In 1904, she and her father George J. Bancroft, who helped construct the area's reservoir system, tied their horses out front and had "a delicious lunch" inside. A photograph of the building taken by Bancroft's father in 1904 appears in her book *Unique Ghost Towns and Mountain Spots*.

Near the Harper cabin is the 1915 Alice School, which operated until 1936. Unfortunately, on my visits the windows were completely covered so I couldn't see the school's unique recreational feature. Because of the long winters, a pipe was installed across the ceiling so that swings could be hung inside.

Beyond Alice on Fall River Road, near the trailhead for St. Mary's Glacier, are several cabins and evidence of mining activity.

When You Go

Alice is 10.6 miles northwest of Idaho Springs. Take Fall River Road from I-70 and go 8.4 miles to Alice Road.

Chapter Three

BRECKENRIDGE GHOSTS

Left: Rolling stock and railroad memorabilia are just two reasons to visit Fairplay's South Park City, one of the West's best outdoor, living-history museums. Other attractions abound as well. Ghost-town enthusiasts will revel in the thousands of gold-rush-era artifacts that are on display in the historic buildings.

Above: Breckenridge is known primarily as a tourist area today, but these rusted, worn household items and the weathered log cabin behind them remind visitors that the town's past wasn't so glamorous.

When you pass through the Eisenhower Tunnel on I-70, you will have the unusual experience of passing *beneath* the Continental Divide. More unusual experiences await you on the back roads of the areas described in this chapter, including two quite rare sights: an arrastra (a crude milling device) in its original location and the remains of an antique dredge. In addition, you can visit a terrific assemblage of western buildings at wonderful South Park City. The average elevation of this chapter's sites is 10,123 feet, the highest average for those in any chapter in this book.

Breckenridge

When prospectors crossed the Continental Divide in the summer of 1859 and started placer diggings on the Blue River, they probably didn't care that they had entered Utah Territory. But they certainly cared that they had entered the Ute Indians' territory. As a result, miners built a crude stockade, calling it Fort Meribeh, reportedly for the only woman in the area, Mary Bigelow ("Mary B"). The Utes, however, were friendly, and the fort was abandoned in favor of a town a mile south. Citizens seeking a post office heard that politics could speed the process, so they chose the name Breckinridge, for then–Vice President John C. Breckinridge. The ploy worked, but when Abraham Lincoln was elected president, Breckinridge defected to the Confederacy. The Unionists in town insisted on changing the spelling to "Breckenridge."

Placer deposits gave out in the 1860s, and the town dried up. In the early 1880s, however, improved quartz mining methods brought miners back.

In 1898, a new mining technique came to Breckenridge, changing the topography forever. Ben Stanley Revett introduced the Blue River to "boat mining," more commonly known as dredging. This technique worked the worn-out placer deposits in ways previously unknown. "Bucket lines" would dredge up huge quantities of gravel, then wash and screen it. Two dredges sat behind Breckenridge's main street, growling and shuddering with such a racket that people would awaken in the night unnerved by the silence if the dredges broke down.

The dredges wreaked environmental havoc, turning up stream beds and leaving huge piles of gravel that still line the banks of the Blue River and nearby French Gulch. The piles were tolerated

Breckenridge's historic buildings are sandwiched among modern hotels and condos that cater to skiers who enjoy the nearby slopes. The overall effect is of a lovely, vibrant town.

because they were the difference between paychecks and poverty. When the dredges shut down during World War II, Breckenridge died.

In 1962, Breckenridge found the gold supply that never seems to end: tourism. A ski area opened on nearby Peak Eight, and the town has basked in a prosperity that mining never approached. Now, with skiers and snowboarders in the winter and mountain bikers in the summer, Breckenridge enjoys a year-round tourist season.

Although high-rise hotels and condominiums dwarf the town's old buildings, its history is still on display in its many old businesses, churches, and residences—and in its towering piles of gravel along the Blue.

Walking and Driving Around Breckenridge
The Summit County Historical Society, at 309 North Main Street, has walking tour guides, brochures, and in-

Early prospectors dreamed of finding placer gold of this quality and quantity.

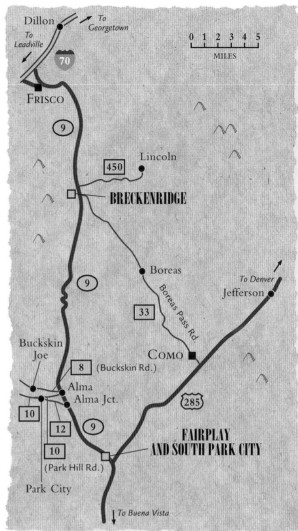

formation. South on Main are the best historic commercial buildings on either side of Lincoln Avenue, including a stone building with a brick facade, built in 1885, at 120 South Main. It is unusual because most older buildings in town are made of wood.

Many lovely residences on High and French Streets, east of Main, have historic markers. Note the elegant 1880s clapboard home at 100 High Street; when it was built, skeptics considered it too far from town for commuting on foot.

Also visit the 1880 Father Dyer Methodist Church at Wellington and Briar Rose Road, and, behind it, a cabin in which he once lived that was moved to this location. Father John Lewis Dyer was a circuit-riding "snowshoe" preacher as well known for his ability to "dowse" for gold as for his ability to deliver sermons. He also performed an important service for his far-flung parishes—in addition to preaching the gospel, he carried the mail.

Breckenridge's Valley Brook Cemetery is north of town. Take Main Street past the traffic light at North Park and turn left on Valley Brook Street.

The cemetery has hundreds of graves. Northwest of the rear of a wooden building are two lovely, nearly identical headstones. Each features a tree stump with two new leaves growing from each stump—a symbol of life over death. Each stone has a child lying on a stump, covered by a shawl. They are for sisters Eugenia and Clara Keller. The epitaph for Eugenia (1893–1895) reads: "Budded on Earth to bloom in Heaven." For Clara (1897–1899), the stone reads: "The choicest flowers bloom to fade."

When You Go

Breckenridge is 14 miles south of Frisco on State Route 9. Frisco is 26 miles southwest of Georgetown on I-70.

Frisco

Frisco came to life in 1873. Founded by miner Henry A. Recsen, it was named by the town's future mayor, Henry Learned. Learned simply nailed a sign that read "Frisco City" to Recsen's cabin. The name was likely a nod to

California's San Francisco, made by someone who didn't realize that citizens there detest the nickname.

The tiny settlement became a town with the arrival of the narrow-gauge tracks of the Denver, South Park & Pacific Railroad, which reached Breckenridge in September 1883, pushed past Frisco into Tenmile Canyon, and completed its route into Leadville in December 1884. Frisco thus became an important supply center and could boast of a saw mill, several stores, and two hotels.

Area mines produced in varying stages of activity until 1918. During the Depression, Frisco's population dropped to less than two dozen. Now, however, steady streams of tourists come to Frisco and nearby ski resorts.

Frisco's modern buildings obscure its few historic ones as you drive along Main Street, until you reach Frisco Historic Park at Second Street at Main. There you will find several excellent buildings, most brought to this site for preservation. The schoolhouse, constructed in about 1890 and in its original location, features displays and a helpful walking tour booklet. Other buildings include an 1881 jail, a log chapel, and several residences.

The 1882 post office–general store is located at 510 Main, while the best historic residences are found one block north on Galena.

The ruins of several 1880s charcoal kilns stand along the Frisco-to-Breckenridge bike route on the southeast side of town. (For directions to similar kilns in far better shape, see the introduction to chapter five.)

The Frisco Cemetery is a few yards east of Main and Summit toward the marina. There are dozens of unmarked or "unknown" graves, along with many markers from the 1930s to the present. I found only one marked grave of antiquity, that of Katy Thomas, who died in 1889 at the age of eighteen months.

When You Go
Frisco is 14 miles north of Breckenridge on State Route 9 and 26 miles southwest of Georgetown on I-70.

Lincoln

The primary reason to journey along French Creek is not for the sparse remains of Lincoln, but rather for a nearby historic remnant. Sitting in a self-created bog is the partially burned, partially salvaged, partially submerged Reiling Dredge. Despite its sorry state, it still has a regal look, almost like a stranded old Mississippi riverboat.

French Gulch placer gold was panned in the 1860s and dredged in the 1900s. In between, gold lodes were

The decaying remains of the Reiling Dredge sit in its own pool along French Creek near Lincoln.

found in the surrounding hills, most notably on Farncomb Hill. Located east of Lincoln, this hill was named for discoverer Harry Farncomb, who found delicate strands of crystallized gold in the 1860s.

A town of fifteen hundred in the 1880s, Lincoln declined in the 1890s, and even the later dredging operations couldn't save it.

Today, Lincoln includes a modern house and two old buildings posted against trespassing. Beyond the town .3 of a mile is the grave of William Milner, who died at age twenty-four in 1864. His is the earliest marked grave I found in the Breckenridge area.

To see the dredge, retrace your route from Lincoln back toward Breckenridge for almost .7 of a mile. Look on your right for a US West green telephone box with the number 3001. Directly across from that box is a side road heading toward the creek. Leave your vehicle along the main road and walk to the dredge, the top part of which is visible from that main road.

When You Go

Lincoln is 4.3 miles northeast of Breckenridge. From downtown, head north on State Route 9. Go past the traffic light for North Park .2 of a mile and take the first turn east onto County Road 450, which becomes Reiling Road. Continue to the intersection of Reiling and Wellington Roads. Turn left, which is Reiling, and go 3 miles to Lincoln.

The townspeople of Alma pose amid the rubble that mining creates. They are perched on a narrow track that likely led away from a mine adit. The men in the foreground display the tools of their trade. Unusual in the photograph is the presence of women and children, as families were rather rare in small mining towns. (Photo by T. C. Miller. Courtesy of the Ted Kierscey Photo Collection.)

Alma, Buckskin Joe, Park City, and Alma Junction

Alma

According to historian Maxine Benson, Alma was named for Alma James, wife of the town's first merchant; or Alma Graves, wife of the owner of the Alma Mine; or Alma Trevor, the first child born there; or Alma Jaynes, daughter of a pioneer. I think it is possible they chose the name because every woman there was named Alma.

Mining in the area began in the 1860s with the for-

mation of the Mosquito District, so called because miners at a meeting there could not agree on a name and adjourned. Reconvening the next day, they found a mashed mosquito in the official ledger, took it as a sign, and agreed on Mosquito.

Alma existed because of prospectors who came over Mosquito Pass in 1872 looking for riches. They went east of the Mosquito District and eventually settled Alma. By the 1880s, several hundred people were living in town, with many more in nearby camps. The town became the area's refining center, but when the silver bonanza hit Leadville, Alma emptied.

Alma today features several historic buildings. The 1936 Alma Community Church is on the State Historic Register. On Buchanan Street is the 1928 Mission-style town hall, formerly the school. A tiny museum in the old fire house features an 1882 horse-drawn fire engine. A particularly lovely two-story frame residence, formerly the St. Nicholas Hotel, stands one block west of the highway on Pine Street.

When in use, this arrastra near Buckskin Joe was not water filled. An arrastra is extremely rare to find in its original location, because many have been moved to museums and, alas, to people's backyards.

Buckskin Joe

Buckskin Joe was west of Alma. (Note: Do not confuse this site with the tourist town near the Royal Gorge that has appropriated its name.) Take County Road 8, which is Buckskin Road in Alma, west for 1.6 miles to the site. The brochure "Buckskin Gulch" will make this drive more enjoyable (see page 51 for information).

Buckskin Joe was founded in 1860 and named for Joe Higganbottom—known as "Buckskin Joe" for his deer-skin clothes—who found the first placer deposits. A gold lode, the Phillips, was discovered in 1861and yielded a half million dollars in two short years. The town received a post office in 1861 under the name of Laurette, a combination of Laura and Jeannette, the names of the only two women in town. That name didn't stick, however, and in 1865 the post office name was changed to Buckskin, which it remained until it closed in 1873. The county seat from 1862 until 1867, Buckskin Joe was home to several thousand people.

Even when pioneer ghost town writer and artist Muriel Sibell Wolle visited Buckskin Joe more than seventy years ago, there was virtually nothing left. No buildings currently stand at the site, but two attractions she mentions in her classic *Stampede to Timberline* are still nearby: the town cemetery and an arrastra.

The turnoff to the Buckskin Joe Cemetery is actually before the townsite. On the south side of the road is a chain link fence protecting Alma's water supply. The first turn north, .1 of a mile beyond that fence, goes to the cemetery. Follow the main dirt road for .4 of a mile up a hill.

A sign proclaims this the Town of Alma Cemetery, established by order of President Roosevelt in 1902. It has been a cemetery much longer than that. The oldest grave I found dated from 1866, when Buckskin Joe, not Alma, was thriving.

The most famous story about Buckskin Joe involves this cemetery. The loveliest woman in town was a saloon dancer known only as Silver Heels for her fancy shoes. When a smallpox epidemic overtook the town, she stayed when others fled, nursing the sick and comforting the dying. She eventually caught the disfiguring disease, but upon recovery, she disappeared. For many years a mysterious, veiled woman occasionally visited the cemetery, placing wildflowers on graves of smallpox victims. Her kindness was not forgotten; rising northeast of Alma is 13,822-foot Mount Silverheels.

One mile beyond the site of Buckskin Joe on County Road 8, at a spot marked by a "wagon wheel" sign #3, is a marvelous arrastra about six feet in diameter, created

Minor changes in row housing often revealed the hierarchy in employment. This lone bay window at Alma Junction probably signifies that its occupant was of higher rank than the residents of the other houses. These small homes were likely built for Denver, South Park & Pacific Railroad workers.

from a large rock from the bank of Buckskin Creek. Arrastras were early milling devices that used a horse, mule, or ox to pull a heavy boulder in a circle to crush ore.

The Paris Mill, posted against trespassing, stands .2 of a mile beyond the arrastra. The road deteriorates beyond the mill, but it is still quite passable for a car under normal conditions. The road continues into an absolutely lovely valley. I recommend going at least 1.3 miles beyond the Paris Mill to see the Sweet Home Mine before turning around. The best rhodochrosite crystals in the world were once found at the Sweet Home. An eight-by-ten-foot wall containing more than three thousand crystals from the mine is displayed at the Denver Museum of Natural History.

Park City

On the south end of Alma is Park Hill Road (County Road 10). Take this road west for .9 of a mile to the Park City Cemetery, which stands on a hill in a clearing south of the road. Several recently placed crosses, a fence, and a solitary headstone make up the site. The stone is for Leola Noel, who died in 1883 at one year. Her epitaph reads: "Our Darling Sleeps."

Park City is 1.7 miles past the cemetery. Once a small collection of cabins surrounding a stagecoach stop along the route to Leadville over Mosquito Pass, Park City today has several attractive roadside log cabins. (Note: if you wish to proceed west from Park City, use the helpful brochure "Mosquito Pass." See page 51).

Alma Junction

Instead of returning to Alma the way you came, take the right fork east of Park City onto County Road 12. In two miles you will arrive at Alma Junction. This town was a railroad terminus for a spur that brought ore from the London Mine, west of Park City, to a branch of the Denver, South Park & Pacific that ended here. You will have been driving part of that railroad grade.

A cabin and a long, narrow frame house stand north of the road, with five wood-frame row houses across the street. The Alma topographic map shows the old railroad grade forming a wye (a Y-shaped track) near the highway at this point; you can still see that old grade.

When You Go

Alma is 15 miles south of Breckenridge and 5 miles north of Fairplay on State Route 9. Refer to the text for directions to the other sites in this section.

Fairplay and South Park City

Fairplay

When prospectors came to the early South Park diggings at Tarryall (see the Jefferson entry later in this chapter), they found miners there in no mood to share and so nicknamed the place "Grab-all." When they moved on and found placer gold in the South Platte River, the men wanted a counter to "Grab-all" for their new diggings and decided upon "Fair Play" in rebuke. The post office opened in that name in the summer of 1861.

In 1869, Fair Play became South Park City, but the name lasted only five years. In 1924, Fair Play was shortened to one word by the U.S. Postal Service.

When placer deposits on the South Platte gave out, miners fanned out looking for primary veins. Although the veins were found several miles away, Fairplay still was

The buildings of South Park City demonstrate common construction materials. Early camps used hewn logs (the buildings in the far background). They were often replaced by sawn-lumber false-front structures (right and center). Only towns with real permanence (or experience with fires) graduated to cut stone or brick buildings with touches like an ornamental cornice (left rear).

Above: *A moment frozen in time at the South Park City depot—wagons with no horses wait while a baggage cart stands on the platform for a train that will never arrive.*

Left: *The seamstress who worked at this 1879 Singer sewing machine in South Park City could glance up from her work to see the unusual decorative touch of cut-log paneling.*

the supply and social center, permanently taking the Park County seat away from Buckskin Joe in 1866. But as the gold deposits faded, Fairplay went into decline.

In the 1870s, the mining emphasis switched to silver when newly discovered deposits brought a resurgence to Fairplay and nearby Alma.

When dredging came to Breckenridge and French Gulch, it wasn't long before the new technique was utilized in Fairplay. When Muriel Sibell Wolle visited the town in 1942, a dredge was busy two miles away. She remarked that, despite its distance from the town, she could still hear it "shrieking and clanging." Those dredging operations left extensive gravel piles along the river. The piles are particularly visible from the north end of town.

50

Fairplay today offers several historic buildings. On Main Street is the library, formerly the 1874 Park County Courthouse. Inside, a wooden spiral staircase leads to the courtroom, but at this writing that room looks more like the 1970s than the 1870s, with paneled walls and orange and brown checkered carpeting. The downstairs features a huge safe from the Mosler Bank Safe Company of Cincinnati.

Next to the former courthouse is the two-cell jail. The mechanism to close the cells is stamped 1874, the year the jail was constructed. South of the old courthouse is the Fairplay Hotel, rebuilt in 1922 after fire destroyed the 1873 original.

On Hathaway, east of the library, stands the Masonic Lodge. At Sixth and Hathaway is the 1874 Sheldon Jackson Chapel, a lovely board-and-batten church with an elaborate belfry. (Reverend Jackson, its namesake, organized many Presbyterian congregations in Colorado.)

Down the street from the chapel is the 1880 school, an attractive two-story stone structure, which, unfortunately, has some plain brick additions that conflict with the original design.

A modern building worth noting is the realty office at Sixth and Main, which is a replica of the depot that once stood in Hancock (see page 96).

To visit the Fairplay Cemetery, go to the junction of State Route 9, U.S. 285, and County Road 16 south of town. Head south from that light on County Road 16. Before it enters private property, take a sharp left up to the cemetery. From there you will have a stunning view west to the Mosquito Range. Because the cemetery is still in use, old graves are mixed in with newer ones. You can drive through much of the cemetery, and there is a northern exit that comes out onto U.S. 285.

The Pike National Forest South Park Ranger District Headquarters has four valuable brochures for this area: "Boreas Pass," "Buckskin Gulch," "Placer Valley," and "Mosquito Pass." The office is located north of U.S. 285 and east of State Route 9.

South Park City

South Park City, one of the West's best outdoor, living-history museums, is located in Fairplay. It was opened to the public in 1959, the centennial of the Pikes Peak Gold Rush. It features a remarkable collection of thirty-four buildings, seven at their original locations and the remainder moved from nearby communities to form a historic town.

Not only are the buildings wonderful, what's inside them is as well. All ghost-town enthusiasts dream of finding an empty town filled with artifacts that citizens left behind. South Park City is the incarnation of that dream. Some sixty thousand items pertinent to the buildings are on display. A one-room, 1879 schoolhouse, with its belfry-capped vestibule, features a complete classroom. The 1880 Bank of Alma retains its teller cages and safe. Merriam's City Drug Store has an astonishing array of patent remedies still in their wrappers. The price of admission to South Park City is very reasonable.

When You Go

Fairplay is 5 miles south of Alma and 20 miles south of Breckenridge on State Route 9. It is also 9 miles west of Como on U.S. 285.

Como

Coal, not the placer gold found earlier in nearby Tarryall Creek, was what brought Italian miners to this area in 1871. They named the town they settled and a tiny nearby lake for their native Como. By 1879 Como was a tent

The Odd Fellows Hall in Como, built in the mid-1880s, features a modest cornice on the front and an unusual, twelve-sided turret that was added in the 1950s.

Above: *This view of the Como roundhouse was taken just a few years after its construction in 1881. The boiler house, with its smokestack and steam vent, appears at the left side of the picture. At its largest, the roundhouse had nineteen bays, including the six shown here. Note that the locomotive at left has a large blade snowplow attached to the front. This plow was one of many used to try to keep the tracks clear in the long winter months. (Photo by George Mellon. Courtesy of the collection of Greg Kazel.)*

Right: *A Denver, South Park & Pacific freight and passenger train stops in 1884 at the original Baker Tank, the only water stop between Breckenridge and Boreas Pass. The current tank at the spot is a replacement installed in 1910 that once stood between Quartz and the Alpine Tunnel (see chapter six). (Photo by W. H. Jackson. Courtesy of the Ted Kierscey Photo Collection.)*

Facing page: *The Como roundhouse is currently undergoing a thorough restoration that began in 1984, including reinstalling a narrow-gauge turntable.*

city of construction workers for the Denver, South Park & Pacific Railroad. The town was a temporary terminus before tracks were extended to Gunnison via the Alpine Tunnel (see chapter six). The railroad's grand plan was to reach the Pacific Ocean, but Gunnison became its western-most terminus. A second rail route was later built over Boreas Pass (see the following entry) from Como to Breckenridge and Leadville.

The railroad's branching at Como increased the town's importance. A roundhouse, depot, and division repair shops served the railroad, while three hotels, brothels, Chinese laundries, shops, and saloons provided for travelers and the town's six hundred residents.

The decline of Como began in 1910 when the Alpine Tunnel route was closed, eliminating much of the rail traffic through town.

The premier building in Como today is Colorado's last narrow-gauge, cut-stone roundhouse. The 1881 six-bay roundhouse stands on the right as you enter town from the south.

A two-story, wood-frame hotel, once the Como Eating House, sits on the site of the Pacific Hotel, which

Above: *This peaceful view of the railroad section house and nearby log cabin gives no hint of the severe weather that occurs frequently at Boreas Pass.*

Right, top: *This 1900 rotary snowplow stands near the beginning of Boreas Pass Road in Breckenridge. Winter snows frequently required plows like this one, because snow sometimes so obscured the tracks that only the tops of telegraph poles showed the route. The plow's steam power only served to rotate the huge blades. To move down the track, the snowplow needed a push from as many as five locomotives to clear the steeper grades.*

Right, bottom: *An earlier version of a rotary snowplow appears in this illustration from* Harper's Weekly *in 1890. Passengers on trains waiting for the plows to clear a path were often so bored that they assisted in shoveling.*

burned in 1896. The current hotel is open for business and serves meals. Next to it is what appears to be a wooden shed but is actually the former depot. Across the street is a 1910 brick building that originally was a saloon, but during and after Prohibition, it served as a mercantile.

On the west side of town is the 1880s schoolhouse, which has been the Como Civic Center since the 1930s. Next to it stands the 1882 Catholic church and rectory.

The Como Cemetery is .4 of a mile north of town. At first glance, this pleasant graveyard appears to contain only a few dozen graves in a clearing, but closer inspection shows that the nearby grove of aspens contains approximately two hundred more. One lovely headstone for Daisy Stark, who died in 1887 at age thirteen, features, appropriately, several carved daisies.

When You Go

Como is .6 of a mile north of U.S. 285 on Road 33, from a point 9 miles east of Fairplay and 7 miles west of Jefferson.

Boreas

Most of the route over Boreas Pass is actually the roadbed of the Denver, South Park & Pacific Railroad, constructed between 1880 and 1884. This rail line connected Denver to the silver bonanza in Leadville via Como, Breckenridge, and Frisco. The construction of the line from Como was a remarkable feat, since the route, which consisted of slightly less than sixty-four miles, contained 435 curves. The longest straight stretch of track was a mere 1.6 miles. The route was taken over by the Colorado & Southern in 1889, which used the tracks until 1937. Because it was a railroad bed, the road is suitable for cars and is an excellent route to see back-country

Colorado without a high-clearance vehicle.

Boreas, aptly named for the Norse god of the north wind, once had a telegraph office, a stone engine house with a turntable and water tank inside, and a post office, reputed to be at the highest elevation in the country.

Only two of Boreas's buildings still stand. One is the railroad section house, which was nearly in ruins when I first saw it in 1988, but which has since been restored. The other is a log cabin that predates the railroad, when the route was a wagon and stagecoach road.

Although the view is timelessly lovely, the area around the pass is noticeably barren. This barrenness is not all due to nature, as you can see by the old stumps covering the hillsides.

Baker Tank is 3.4 miles beyond the pass. Restored in 1958 and again in 1991, this water tank was moved from the roadbed near the Alpine Tunnel in 1910 (see page 89).

When You Go
Boreas is 10 miles southeast of Breckenridge and 10 miles northwest of Como. From Como, take Road 33. From Breckenridge, take Boreas Pass Road, the first turn east after the traffic light at Main and South Park. You will enjoy the route between Como and Breckenridge much more with the brochure "Boreas Pass," available in Fairplay (see page 51).

Jefferson

Pikes Peak argonauts were frustrated that they were located within four separate territories—Kansas, Nebraska, Utah, and New Mexico—each with distant government seats. Eager to shape their own destiny but with no authority whatsoever, they formed their own territory in 1859, calling it Jefferson. While only Congress can create a territory, "Jefferson" did set Congress into motion. Many in Congress, however, balked at the name, believing that only the first U.S. president deserved to have a state named after him. Others considered Thomas Jefferson, as founder of the Democratic Party, too political a figure.

Congress granted statehood to Kansas in January 1861 with its present western boundary. The next month, it signed a bill creating a new territory called Colorado. The area was named for the river, which, ironically, was not within its boundaries. (In Colorado Territory the river was officially called Grand River until 1921.)

All of this is to introduce a tiny settlement that stayed true to the non-territory and non-state of Jefferson. Located on the eastern edge of a broad valley known as South Park, Jefferson was a supply center for nearby min-

The graceful bell tower of the Jefferson Community Church is reflected in a puddle after an early morning shower.

ing at Tarryall, Hamilton, and Georgia Gulch. Its permanence was established when the Denver, South Park & Pacific Railroad built a depot in the early 1880s, on the route between Denver and Como.

That depot still stands adjacent to the highway and is one of two particularly delightful buildings in Jefferson. The other is the community church, one block south of town. The town also features several attractive wood-frame residences and a log cabin.

Five miles west of Jefferson is a sign denoting the Tarryall Diggings. These man-made hillocks that head off to the northwest are the remains of the sluice tailings where approximately $2 million in gold was found beginning in 1859.

When You Go
Jefferson is 16 miles northeast of Fairplay on U.S. 285. It is also 7 miles northeast of Road 33, the turnoff to Como, on U.S. 285.

Chapter Four

LEADVILLE GHOSTS

Left: *Holy Cross City offers what dedicated back-roads enthusiasts seek—a remote ghost town in truly spectacular high-country scenery.*

Above: *The piles of waste dumps and the denuded slopes of Leadville in 1890 show that great riches have already been extracted from the area, but this miner is involved in a distinctly small-time operation with a tiny, bare-bones headframe. (Photo by Graves Photo. Courtesy of the Ted Kierscey Photo Collection.)*

For years, Leadville was a rather seedy place that tourists drove through en route to fashionable destinations such as Aspen and Breckenridge. It has improved considerably, but it retains just enough tarnish to keep it a delightful place to prowl around.

Also in this chapter is Holy Cross City, one of Colorado's most obscure ghost towns, and Vicksburg and Winfield, two quaint back-roads sites. Red Cliff stands, overlooked, near a main highway. Finally, Gilman is one of Colorado's more photogenic ghost towns, but because it is a private town closed to the public, you will have to gawk from the road.

As you visit the sites described in this chapter, you will be surrounded by magnificent scenery. Of the state's fifty-three "Fourteeners" (peaks fourteen thousand feet and higher), thirty are within fifty miles of Leadville.

Leadville

Leadville is legendary for its triumphs and tragedies. In 1860, a group of prospectors discovered placer gold in what they optimistically named California Gulch. The camp they founded was also named in hopeful expectation: Oro City. The gulch gave up a few million dollars in gold before its placers played out and people drifted away. In the late 1860s, a quartz lode was developed at the Printer Boy Mine, but again the excitement was short lived.

In the summer of 1877, however, a real bonanza was discovered around the corner from Oro City. The strike was not gold, but silver. Leadville, named for the lead carbonate in which the ore was found, came to life two miles northwest of Oro City.

The first huge returns came from the Little Pittsburg Mine early in 1878. Its riches began the storied rise—and eventual fall—of one of Colorado's most famous citizens: Horace Austin Warner Tabor.

Tabor and his wife, Augusta, had arrived in Idaho Springs early in the rush to Clear Creek. While Tabor pursued placer deposits, Augusta opened a bakery. When they later moved to Buckskin Joe, Tabor worked a claim but also opened a grocery store, and his wife took in boarders. Eventually Tabor became the post-

Leadville in 1881 may have had muddy, rut-filled streets, but it also could claim the then two-year-old Tabor Opera House, the tallest building on this stretch of Harrison Avenue. (Photo by W. H. Jackson. Courtesy of the Ted Kierscey Photo Collection.)

master of Buckskin Joe. The couple's businesses, not their mining claims, paid their bills.

Later, they went to Oro City, and then Leadville, where the Tabors again had a store. A highly respected citizen, Horace was elected Leadville's first mayor. In addition to his official duties and his store, he occasionally grubstaked prospectors.

Among the prospectors to whom Tabor gave supplies were George Hook and August Rische, who by sheer chance (legend says they selected where to dig because it was in the shade) found a silver vein that became the Little Pittsburg. Tabor's share made him rich. From there he seemed to make one uncanny financial investment after another until he was one of the West's wealthiest multimillionaires, lavishly spending vast sums and financing, among other projects, Leadville's Tabor Grand Hotel and Tabor Opera House.

Elizabeth McCourt Doe was called "Baby Doe" by admiring miners in Black Hawk. A divorcée when she came to Leadville, she met Horace Tabor in an elegant restaurant. Their subsequent relationship, secret marriage,

Balance scales were used to weigh gold. In many mining communities, gold was used as the initial medium of exchange.

Worthless ore sits in a car near a headframe at the Matchless Mine. Behind to the left is the shack in which Baby Doe Tabor froze to death in 1935.

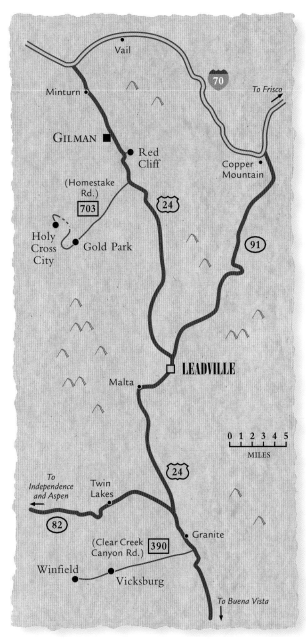

and his divorce from his faithful wife Augusta scandalized the Colorado social scene. (Augusta was given $300,000 in the divorce settlement—a paltry sum, considering that the Tabors were worth an estimated $9.4 million.)

Tabor and Baby Doe lived in high style until overspending, ill-advised investments, and the 1893 Silver Crash brought them to financial ruin. They who had once reigned over Leadville left for the obscurity of Ward. In 1898, Tabor was granted an appointment as Denver's postmaster. He died there, destitute, the following year.

Before he died, Tabor advised Baby Doe that whatever she did, she should hold onto a Leadville mine called the Matchless. Though worthless at the time, he was convinced this mine would eventually pay off and solve the couple's financial woes. Baby Doe returned to Leadville, remembering her husband's deathbed advice, and moved into a tiny shack at the deserted and run-down Matchless operation.

Baby Doe became a proud but pathetic figure in Leadville, "paying" for necessities with worthless promissory notes to sympathetic shopkeepers and refusing the charity offered by others. In March 1935, after a particularly heavy snowstorm, people grew concerned that they had not seen her. They found her frozen body, clad in rags, on the floor of her cabin.

Incidentally, Augusta Tabor, although bitter and hurt by her divorce, carefully invested her settlement. When she died in 1895 at the age of sixty-two, she left an estate of about $1.5 million, making her one of Denver's wealthiest women.

In its history, Colorado has produced more silver than any other state. Leadville alone was responsible for an astonishing one-third of that total, an estimated $113 million.

The Silver Crash of 1893 nearly doomed the city, but it hung on with the discovery of gold in the Little Jonny Mine in the 1890s. In 1901, lead and zinc production kept the town alive. During Prohibition, Leadville's countless mine shafts hid stills that supplied liquor to Denver. During World War II, the construction of Camp Hale

Above: *The Mining Museum Hall of Fame, located in the old high school, has fine displays such as the Gold Rush Room, a blacksmith shop, and a reproduction "underground" mine tunnel.*

Right: *Leadville's Healy House is an elaborate 1878 clapboard home complete with posh Victorian furniture and interesting household items.*

beyond Tennessee Pass created hundreds of jobs, and for a while Leadville's hotels, boarding houses, trailers, and even its former brothels were completely occupied. Later, molybdenum mining at nearby Climax helped the Leadville economy. Everything after 1893, however, has been stopgap. Leadville's true glory days ended more than a century ago.

Walking and Driving Around Leadville

An annual "Summer Guide," widely available in town, can help you enjoy Leadville. The Heritage Museum, located in the 1904 Carnegie Library on the north end of downtown, is a good place to start a tour of the town, because it has an easy-to-follow history of Leadville with a sequential display of dioramas, photographs, and text.

Many historic buildings stand along the highway through Leadville. That road is Harrison Avenue, named for founding father Edwin Harrison, president of a refining and smelting company.

The Tabor Opera House, located on Harrison near Third Street, is a building not to miss. Constructed by Horace Tabor in 1879 in a mere hundred days, it was set for demolition in 1955. It was saved when Florence Hollister and her daughter Evelyn Furman bought it and began the preservation of the structure. Florence has since died, but Evelyn still takes your admission in the foyer, except on Saturday, when the opera house is closed.

The Western Hardware Company is on the corner of Harrison and Fifth. Inside you will find lots of antique items, including some mementos from Camp Hale. The

antique storage bins and ornate display cases filled with old-time knick-knacks are worth the visit. (Many items are not for sale, however.) Be sure to go upstairs to see where lodgers once lived.

The east side of town contains several commercial and public buildings, including false-front stores on the northeast corner of Sixth and Poplar. At Seventh and Poplar is the Annunciation Catholic Church, constructed over a period of years beginning in 1879. Its off-center bell tower is said to have the highest spire in the country, beginning as it does at ten thousand feet elevation.

On Seventh Street east of Hemlock stands the Colorado & Southern depot, now the departure point for a scenic rail ride. The train is diesel powered, unlike the major tourist lines in Colorado. And, unlike the others, it essentially parallels a highway, State Route 91 between Leadville and Climax (albeit at a higher vantage point). In the depot's parking lot stands a beautiful 1906 locomotive that I would love to see pulling the train.

From the depot, you can head east on Seventh for almost a mile to the famous Matchless Mine. If you are interested in the saga of the Tabors, this is an important stop. You can stand where the body of the penniless Baby Doe was found, still heeding her deceased husband's advice to hold on to the Matchless. I found the experience quite moving. Baby Doe, incidentally, was not buried in Leadville but next to her husband in Denver.

To reach the cemeteries of Leadville, go west on Eighth from Harrison. Turn right at James, then left at the fork

The prominent placement of his name on his opera house testifies that Horace Tabor did not do things quietly. Consider how much more attractive the edifice would have been without the lettering.

Leadville's imposing and rather eerie 1879 hospital stands vacant at Tenth Street and Hemlock. Originally operated by the Sisters of Charity, it closed in the 1960s.

The Tabor Opera House is an enchanting place to visit as you explore the balcony, dressing rooms, and backstage area. And when you venture onto the stage itself, you will be standing where legendary performers such as Oscar Wilde, Harry Houdini, and John Philip Sousa once stood.

in the road. At Tenth and James, you will see the Evergreen Cemetery.

This cemetery, like most larger ones in the West, is sectioned off. A sign directs you to areas for Masons, Elks, Odd Fellows, the Ancient Order of United Workmen, and a poignant section called Baby Land.

To visit the St. Joseph Catholic Cemetery, drive south from Evergreen Cemetery on Tenth. Turn right at McWethy; the cemetery will be on your left.

When You Go

Leadville is 24 miles southwest of Interstate 70 on State Route 91 and 37 miles north of Buena Vista on U.S. 24. (Note: A quaint schoolhouse, the only historic remnant of Malta, is about 4 miles southwest of Leadville on U.S. 24.)

Holy Cross City

Holy Cross City sits abandoned along one of the most treacherous roads I've ever seen. When photographer John Drew and I left our four-wheel-drive vehicle behind and trekked to the site, we passed two highly modified backroads vehicles. We made better time hiking than they did driving.

Holy Cross City was named for Mount of the Holy Cross, a peak three miles to the north that has a snowfield somewhat in the shape of a cross. The community and its downhill sister Gold Park, now merely a site along Homestake Road, came into being about the same time as Leadville. In 1881, Gold Park had a population of four hundred. A daily stage brought the mail from Leadville to Gold Park; from there it was carried two thousand feet higher in about 2.5 steep miles to Holy Cross City. At its peak, Holy Cross City had a population of about three hundred and featured a mill, boarding house, assay office, justice of the peace, school, general merchandise, post office, and several cabins. It also had an iron flume that carried ore down to Gold Park. (A flume was an open, man-made trough

that carried water or water-based materials from one location to another using gravity.)

By 1883 the ores had played out. By the end of that year, the population was one family—mining company manager H. W. Roby, his wife, and their children.

How can one be objective about such a place as Holy Cross City? After a hike of about two miles and a climb of just over a thousand feet, I suppose anything would

Holy Cross City has four log cabins, two under roof and two that are only three to five logs high. At the mill site, below the cabins, is some interesting equipment, including a double furnace or boiler, large wheels, and worm gears. Be wary of nearby mine tunnels.

look good, but for John and me, the place was a treasure. It wasn't really the townsite. The treasure came from the entire experience—the challenging hike, the kaleidoscope of wildflowers, the roaring waterfalls along French Creek, the brisk air, the threatening clouds that did nothing but show off, and the scant remains of Holy Cross City.

When You Go

To reach Holy Cross City, drive north from Leadville on U.S. 24. Fifteen miles from Leadville you will pass the site of Camp Hale, once home to fourteen thousand men of World War II's Tenth Mountain Division, the first and only U.S. soldiers trained for combat as ski and mountain troops.

Beyond the Camp Hale sign 4.1 miles is a turnoff to the west, Homestake Road (Road 703). Follow it for 7.2 miles to the site of Gold Park. From there you can begin the four-wheel-drive trail or, if you want to get as close as you can before you attempt the trail, keep going past Gold Park.

To follow our route, proceed .6 of a mile to Road 704. In almost two miles you will come to a trailhead and a huge water pipe. Keep going for another 1.2 miles, where there is a junction. Take the right fork (the left goes steeply up) and proceed until you can see the four-wheel-drive road approaching on your right as you begin to turn left. Park here and begin your hike on the trail (your road ends at a diversion dam), or, if you have a serious back-roads vehicle, drive up the trail. This is a true four-wheel-drive road, and the boulders that you will have to traverse show lots of scrapes—and lots of oil.

Red Cliff

Mining at the junction of Turkey Creek and the Eagle River brought a tent city to life in 1879 as the Leadville excitement spread in all directions. A post office was granted in 1880 as Red Cliff, named for the nearby bluffs colored by hematite.

That tent city celebrated the erection of a sawmill as if it were a guarantee of permanence. On St. Patrick's Day, the first log was sawn, then tied to the back of a burro and decorated with evergreens in honor of the day. The burro and its festooned board then headed a parade through town. Afterward, everyone got drunk, including the burro.

By the fall of 1881, the town was a railroad stop along the Denver & Rio Grande and featured five hotels, a brass band, and a local acting company.

Despite three fires in only one month in 1883, the

town continued to grow. A community of 250 in 1880, it reached 400 within a few years. Although it did not have spectacular times, it had steady ones. When the last mine closed in 1977, the Red Cliff area had produced paying ore for almost a century.

You enter Red Cliff on what was the old highway prior to construction of the high bridge over the Eagle River. Among the historic structures in town are the 1881 Presbyterian church and, across the street, the combination town hall and volunteer fire department. The Red Cliff School, which now houses a small museum, stands on a hill across the Eagle River.

Consider stopping at the school to see the museum. It takes up only one room of the school, but it is packed with interesting memorabilia, including items from Camp Hale. You will also see old school photos, band uniforms, antique household items, and copies of newspapers dating from the turn of the century.

To reach the cemetery, take Monument to Pine, pass Mount Carmel Church, go behind the school, and take the dirt road directly ahead. The steep but well-maintained route ends at the cemetery, which sits among lovely pines.

When You Go
Red Cliff is 2 miles north of Homestake Road (the turnoff to Holy Cross City) on U.S. 24.

Gilman

Gilman was founded in 1886 by miners who worked there but lived in Red Cliff. Tired of the twice-a-day hike, they created a camp nearer their claims. Variously known as Clinton, Battle Mountain, and Rock Creek, the town became Gilman in honor of Henry M. Gilman, who represented the town's investors.

The primary metal found around Gilman in those days was silver, except at the Ground Hog Mine, which yielded gold in nugget form. The town's population reached three hundred in 1899, but a fire that year destroyed half of the buildings in Gilman, including a hotel, the school, many homes and businesses, and the shaft house of the Bell Mine.

The Empire Zinc Company bought up claims about the time of World War I and centralized them into one large underground mine. To reach it, workers walked a long, zigzagging trail from Gilman down more than seven hundred feet where an entrance stood trackside along the Eagle River.

Gilman became a company town, and many new houses were built in the 1940s as the population rose to about five hundred. The town also featured a barber shop,

A truly unusual sight awaits you on Shrine Pass Road only .6 of a mile east of Red Cliff. There, partially hidden by brush, is a large brick beehive kiln on the far side of Turkey Creek. To reach it, walk across the creek about .1 of a mile back toward town at a spot posted against vehicles.

market, bowling alley, company store, seven-bed hospital, and a clubhouse fashioned from the old opera house. Life was hardly idyllic, however. The mine, one of the lowest paying in the country, suffered from labor strikes. The company ceased zinc production in 1977, but a modest copper and silver operation remained. In 1985, all production discontinued, and the few remaining residents were given ninety-day eviction notices.

In its ninety-nine years of mining, Gilman produced 12.8 million tons of ore, principally zinc, but also lead, copper, silver, and gold.

Gilman today is closed to the public and posted against trespassing. Fences, stout locks, and a caretaker discourage anyone who attempts to enter. According to a former resident, vandals have taken a heavy toll on the buildings.

While I was standing at an overlook gazing longingly at Gilman, I struck up a conversation with a man who was enjoying the same view, but for a different reason. He

Gilman has many potentially habitable homes. A former resident said it was a shame that the town isn't occupied, since inexpensive housing is scarce in the area, especially for people working at Vail, ten miles from Gilman.

told me about what happened to him in 1947, when Gilman was full of life. Then a teenager, he was a passenger in a car driven by a buddy. His friend missed the curve, and the car plummeted toward the mine buildings below. But instead of hitting them, the car rammed the only object in between—a power pole. (When you visit the site, it is the pole nearest the white building with the red roof.) The driver was thrown from the car but was unhurt. My narrator ended up in the well of the back seat wrapped up in a blanket that had been folded on the seat. He had a few bumps on his head but was not seriously hurt. When you see the distance they traveled and the steepness of the hill, you will appreciate how fortunate they were.

Their accident was big news in Gilman. When their car knocked down the pole, it also knocked out the power, shutting down the entire mining operation.

When You Go

To view Gilman, drive 1.5 miles north from the turnoff to Red Cliff on U.S. 24. Gilman is also 6 miles south of I-70.

Vicksburg and Winfield

Vicksburg

Vicksburg was founded in 1879 when gold and silver were discovered along Clear Creek. The town, named for storekeeper Vick Keller, featured a school, two saloons and billiard parlors, two hotels, and a boarding house, along with many log cabin residences. The post office, called Vicksburgh, lasted from 1881 until 1885, about the time the precious metals of the area gave out.

The main road now bypasses Vicksburg, but you can still visit this lovely little town by parking at the Vicksburg Museum's lot and walking in. This way is rather like backing into town, because once you come to the front of the museum, you will also see Vicksburg's main street, shaded by rows of Balm of Gilead trees, which were packed in by burros during the town's heyday. Six well-maintained old cabins, posted against trespassing and privately owned (some by descendants of the original miners) line the north side of the street.

The museum, opened weekends and holidays by the Clear Creek Canyon Historical Society, is located in the Shephard House and recreates a mining-era home. On the museum's grounds are interesting artifacts, such as a tram drum, ore cars, wagons, a smelter pot, and a gold rocker (a device used to separate gold from its surrounding material).

Across the road from the parking lot is the Missouri Gulch Trailhead to the Collegiate Wilderness. If you follow that trail for perhaps ten minutes, you will cross Clear Creek and come to a fenced grave for William Huffman. A sign indicates that William, whose father was a miner and mother ran the boarding house, was born in 1884 and died of pneumonia after only a month. This is the only evidence of the Vicksburg Cemetery, incorrectly labeled as the Winfield Cemetery on the Mount Harvard topographic map. The rest of the cemetery, however much of it there might have been, is completely overgrown.

Winfield

Winfield came to life in the 1860s. Its population peaked in 1890 at about fifteen hundred, when the town consisted of three saloons, two hotels, a post office, newspaper office, blacksmith's shop, and a church that no one ever bothered to attend. The 1893 Silver Crash emptied the town, but there was a modest revival between the early 1900s and the end of World War I.

Nestled in a spectacular valley, Winfield today has about a dozen buildings, all but two apparently of antiquity. The Winfield School is now a museum maintained by the Clear Creek Canyon Historical Society.

West of the school is a residence identified as the 1888 cabin of Harry Payne. Across the street from the school is the Ball Cabin, nicely restored by the historical society. A sign says that the cabin is typical of the ones in Winfield between 1870 and 1915. The building has a dirt floor, log dining table, stove, bed, sewing machine, and a place to wash. It also displays photographs of people and places around Winfield. Included are William Wallace and other members of the Wallace family. If you go to the Winfield Cemetery, you will find William Wallace Jr. buried there.

That cemetery is reached by driving or walking .5 of a mile on the road heading north from the turnaround west of the Payne Cabin.

Approximately twenty-five graves are in the cemetery, the first dating from 1885, according to a sign. Thirteen graves are surrounded by rocks, but it is difficult to ascertain where the other dozen might be. One of the graves is for Harold Payne (1894–1899), who died in a snowslide. I wondered if he was the son of Harry Payne, whose cabin is near the school.

When You Go

Vicksburg is 8.3 miles west of U.S. 24 on Clear Creek Canyon Road (Road 390), which is 1.7 miles south of Granite and 18 miles south of Leadville. Winfield is 3.9 miles west of Vicksburg.

Above: *The 1880s Winfield School is a one-room log building with a clapboard false front, which indicates it probably served a commercial purpose originally.*

Left: *The interior of the Winfield School shows it well equipped for education (and warmth). The school has been restored to its appearance at the turn of the twentieth century.*

Chapter Five

ASPEN GHOSTS

Left: *What is popularly, but erroneously, called the Crystal Mill is one of Colorado's most famous ghost town images.*

Above: *Lit by a single candle lodged in the face of the rock, two Aspen-area miners use a process called "upjacking" to drill holes in which to place explosives. (Courtesy of the Aspen Historical Society.)*

Aspen is so well known as a playground of the rich and famous that most visitors probably don't know it was originally a mining town. It also was once nearly a ghost town.

Other sites discussed in this chapter include Ashcroft and Independence, preserved and protected true ghost towns; Redstone, a planned utopian mining community; Marble, the only quarry town in this book; and Crystal, a small village along a four-wheel-drive road with one of Colorado's most photographed buildings.

Note: Also worth seeing in this area are seven historic beehive ovens standing next to a suburban park in Basalt, 18 miles northwest of Aspen. To see them, turn east from State Route 82 onto Basalt Avenue, south on Two Rivers, and east on Elk Run Drive. The ovens, one nearly whole and the others in various states of decay, can be seen in .7 of a mile.

Aspen

Prospectors who had missed out on Leadville's bonanza climbed Independence Pass and went down into a valley along the Roaring Fork in 1879. They found silver float almost immediately and set up a tent camp they called Ute City.

In the spring of 1880, promoter, town surveyor, and future mayor B. Clark Wheeler came to camp. He re-named the place Aspen before returning to Leadville, where his tales of the new camp began a rush to purchase town plots he had ready to sell.

But the glowing review of the camp was no promoter's exaggeration. Lode silver was found in numerous places on Aspen, Red, and Smuggler Mountains. Some mines produced staggering amounts; in 1883, a bedroom-sized chamber in the Emma Mine produced five hundred thousand dollars alone. That year the country's largest ore body—140 feet across—was discovered in the Compromise Mine.

The Denver & Rio Grande Railroad reached Aspen from Glenwood Springs in 1887, fol-lowed a year later by the Colo-rado Midland, which came from Leadville through the Hager-man Tunnel. Railroads made silver mining much more prof-itable, because they signifi-cantly reduced transportation costs. In 1884, before the rail-

The railroad may have reached Aspen by the time this photo was taken in 1890, but pack animals were still the freight vehicle for the average miner. The bonanza nature of the town is reflected in the construction going on. The real bonanza, however, would be found decades later on the famous ski slopes on the mountains in the background. (Photo by B. W. Kilburn. Courtesy of the Ted Kierscey Photo Collection.)

roads, $3.5 million worth of silver was produced. In 1888, that figure rose to $7 million. A year later it approached $10 million.

Aspen basked in the prosperity. It installed the state's first electric streetlights. Its eight thousand citizens could eat in posh restaurants, entertain guests in the opulent Hotel Jerome, enjoy the refinement of a lavish opera house, and take a "Bathing Train" to the warm waters at Glen-wood Springs.

Then came 1893, the repeal of the Sherman Act, and the precipitous drop in silver's value. Although Aspen was seriously wounded by the Silver Crash, it did not com-pletely collapse as many silver towns did. Miners took wage cuts and Aspen, however tentatively, held on. In fact, one-sixth of all the silver in the United States produced between 1894 and 1918 came from Aspen. In 1894, the Smuggler Mine produced a nugget of 93 percent pure silver and weighing 2,060 pounds. After 1918, however, Aspen came very close to becoming a ghost town. Its primary appeal was to summer visitors who enjoyed its fishing streams and hiking trails.

During World War II, the skiing Tenth Mountain Di-vision, quartered at Camp Hale north of Leadville, trained on Aspen's slopes. In 1945, Chicago industrialist Walter

The Mine Examiner and Prospector's Companion was but one of many books available to inexpe-rienced and veteran prospectors and miners alike.

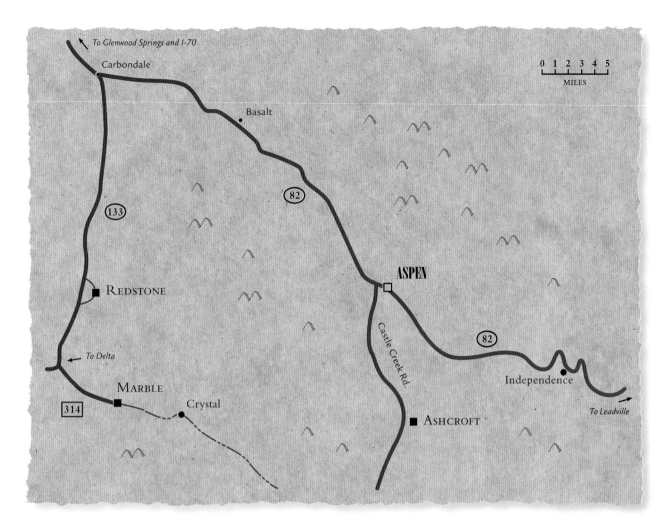

Paepcke and his wife Elizabeth viewed those slopes and saw opportunity. They purchased bargain buildings, many for back taxes, and redecorated the Hotel Jerome. They opened Aspen in 1947 as a ski resort and cultural center. The Paepckes' vision not only saved Aspen but also set a pattern that rescued several other near ghost towns.

Walking and Driving Around Aspen

To get a feel for early-day Aspen, visit the 1888 Wheeler/ Stallard House Museum at 620 West Bleeker Street, where you can take a self-guided tour to see elegant period furniture and memorabilia.

Downtown Aspen contains many old buildings, but because of all the spiffing up they have received, most don't look old. Two fine examples are the 1889 Jerome Hotel, at Mill and Bleeker, and the 1889 Wheeler Opera House, at Mill and Hyman.

Another way to capture Aspen's historic side is to visit its three cemeteries. The Red Butte Cemetery is the largest and the best tended. It is also, for ghost town enthusiasts, the least rewarding, because a large percentage of its headstones are modern. To reach it, take the main highway toward Glenwood Springs. After you cross the bridge over Castle Creek, turn right onto Cemetery Lane and pro-

ceed one mile north.

More difficult to locate is the Ute Cemetery, which sits forgotten and overgrown in the midst of Aspen's luxury. It is symbolic of Aspen's history—it certainly exists, but you have to do some searching. To see this cemetery, go to the intersection of Cooper and Original. Head south on Original, which becomes Ute. Proceed to a parking lot beyond the Ute Place subdivision. You will have just passed the cemetery. Park and return on foot a few yards.

I hope the Ute Cemetery will be better tended than when I was there. No historic place should be so ignored. The nearby bike path is nicely groomed, and the homes surrounding the cemetery are immaculate, but the old headstones stand obliterated by brush and weeds. I discovered ten marked graves and saw evidence of several more that were unmarked. Many headstones were for children. The oldest marker I found was from 1882, only two years after Aspen's birth.

The most interesting and by far the most secluded graveyard is the Aspen Grove Cemetery. To reach it, head east on Cooper toward Independence Pass and turn left on McSkimming Road, .5 of a mile from Original. Turn

71

The lobby of Aspen's elegant Hotel Jerome has an inlaid, carved oak fireplace and mirror. A recent renovation has turned the room into a three-story atrium, so the chandeliers now hang from a false ceiling.

The Hotel Jerome's library-bar features a pressed-tin ceiling and a lovely oak wall piece that includes inset stained glass. The glass table top (center) is supported by a base made of antlers.

The exquisite chandelier in Aspen's Wheeler Opera House originally came from Chicago's Drake Hotel. It was installed during a renovation in the 1950s.

Ashcroft features a variety of construction styles—the assay office (left) has an arching roof, the laundry (center) has a pitched roof, and the post office (right) has a false front.

right onto Aspen Grove Cemetery Road. Park at the end and follow the path for about 175 yards to the cemetery.

If you didn't know a city was so nearby, you might think you were in a lovely, rural spot on the Colorado back roads. Large sections of this aspen-shaded cemetery lie unused, and most graves predate 1900. The farther back into the cemetery you go, the more markers you will discover.

When You Go

Aspen is 42 miles southeast of Glenwood Springs and 59 miles west of Leadville on State Route 82.

Ashcroft

Two prospectors from the new camp called Aspen found silver deposits along Castle Creek and formed their own camp, Castle Forks City, where the two forks of Castle Creek join. The boom year was 1882, when rich ore was found in the Montezuma and Tam O'Shanter mines. The owners received financial backing from Horace Tabor, who had recently become a very rich man in Leadville

(see chapter four). In 1883, when Tabor came with his new bride Baby Doe to inspect his holdings, miners enjoyed a twenty-four-hour celebration that included a ball, banquet, and free drinks in the town's twenty saloons.

By then the place was known as Ashcroft, named—with a slight variation—for prospector and town promoter T. E. Ashcraft, who had actually founded a short-lived competing camp called Highland. Ashcroft had a school, bowling alley, sawmill, smelter, two newspapers, six hotels, and a population of two thousand, making it larger than Aspen.

Ashcroft's ore bodies were quickly depleted, however, and by 1885 many of its buildings had been moved to Aspen, where major silver strikes attracted miners from all over. Ashcroft was a has-been, home to only a hundred summer residents. It was a ghost town by 1900, although the post office hung on for twelve more years, perhaps by bureaucratic oversight.

During World War II, the town was used for ski training by the Tenth Mountain Division from Camp Hale. After World War II, Stuart Mace, commander of the

Independence's log cabins vary from an intact store (center) to a mere skeleton (foreground). Preservation efforts are underway, and an intern who lives on the property provides interpretive talks and guided tours during the warm months of the year.

canine division of the Tenth Mountain Division, returned to Ashcroft to raise and train toklat huskies. Mace and his dogs were featured in the 1950s television series *Sergeant Preston of the Yukon* with Ashcroft often used as the setting for the show.

Today Ashcroft is being protected and restored by the Aspen Historical Society. You can visit this genuine ghost town, enjoy the site, and leave with the feeling that the town will still be there if you return years later. That is, unfortunately, seldom the case.

The two-story Hotel View is the grandest and most photogenic structure in town. Other buildings include cabins, a mercantile, jail, blacksmith's shop, assay office, laundry, and post office.

A saloon is the current headquarters for the historical society, where you will find old photographs, accounts of the town's history, and souvenirs. I enjoyed a reprint of the *Ashcroft Journal* from 1882, which was both informative and amusing.

When You Go

Ashcroft is 12 miles from Aspen. At the second light beyond the Castle Creek Bridge west of town, turn left, followed by a second left onto Castle Creek Road. Ashcroft is 10.8 miles beyond.

Independence

Leadville miner Billy Belden led a group of prospectors over Independence Pass in 1879. Finding good placer deposits in the Roaring Fork River not far beyond the pass, they set up a tent camp and named it Belden. On the Fourth of July of that year, they struck paydirt and named the claim Independence.

The town's name of Belden didn't last long, and new monikers were adopted so regularly that the *Rocky Mountain News* once glibly announced, "This is about the fourth change. It is expected to hold good for a week or ten days." Writer Caroline Bancroft chronicled the changes succinctly, calling the town "Belden-Independence-

A bank of coke ovens stands along the highway near the south entrance to Redstone. The ovens, which date from the 1890s, utilized a slow-burning, controlled-oxygen process to convert charcoal to coke, which is a longer-lasting fuel than coal.

Chipeta-Sidney-Farwell-Sparkhill-Mammoth City-Mount Hope-Chipeta-Independence."

Whatever its name, the town was both a mining camp and a stagecoach layover stop. Within a few years, however, the ore had given out, and the railroad had reached Aspen, making travel over the pass unnecessary. By 1888, the population of Independence was only a hundred. By 1900, only Jack Williams, caretaker of the mill, remained. When he left in 1912, Independence was dead.

Independence today is enjoyable because, like Ashcroft, it is being carefully preserved and cautiously restored by the Aspen Historical Society in cooperation with the U.S. Forest Service.

On the east end of the site are four cabins, ranging from mere foundations to remnants six or seven logs high. In the center of town, three buildings are under roof, and a cabin ruin stands across the Roaring Fork River. A large hewn-log general store serves as town headquarters. Four roofless but restorable cabins stand nearby. The intern's cabin is west of the general store.

West of the townsite .5 of a mile are mill ruins, a hopper, a cabin, and a mine.

When You Go

Independence is 15.5 miles southeast of Aspen and 44 miles southwest of Leadville on State Route 82.

Redstone

Named for its sandstone cliffs, Redstone came to life because of vast coal deposits found in 1884 by John Cleveland Osgood. He and other investors founded the Colorado Fuel and Iron Company, which became an industry giant. Their mines at Coal Basin, four miles west of Redstone, produced more than a million tons of coal.

Osgood was a different brand of capitalist. Instead of taking advantage of underpaid workers, he did quite the opposite, creating Redstone as a model company town with practically utopian conditions. Married men and their families lived in eighty-four Swiss-chalet-style cottages, no two alike. Each two-to-five-room cottage, landscaped with lawns and gardens, had the then-unheard of luxury of electricity and running water. Bachelors lived in a forty-room lodge, now the respected Redstone Inn. Its clubhouse was open to all employees and featured a library and theater, where the company provided drama productions, lectures, and concerts.

His second wife, Alma Regina Shelgram, shared her husband's attitudes toward their employees. Her benevolence to the workers and their families earned her the sobriquet "Lady Bountiful."

Osgood allowed a bit of capitalist's luxury for himself, however. He completed a $2.5 million, forty-two-room mansion in 1902. Called Cleveholm Manor, it had walls covered in hand-tooled leather and was filled with elegant furniture designed specifically for the estate.

When Osgood died in 1926, his third wife sold the estate, and eventually the coal mines closed. When author-artist Muriel Sibell Wolle visited Redstone in 1942, it was almost deserted, and the Redstone Inn had only recently opened. Between 1956 and 1991, Coal Basin operated again, with twenty-eight million tons of coal extracted.

The grand Redstone Inn is the most imposing structure in town. Now on the National Register of Historic Places, it has more than doubled in size since its days as the bachelor quarters.

If you walk north from the inn, you will pass the 1902 school, several original residences, and many tourist-related businesses. A tiny museum, housed in a former lantern house relocated from Coal Basin, has photographs of the town, the Redstone Inn, and Cleveholm Manor. Cleveholm Manor is now a private mountain inn, but tours are occasionally available. The elegant mansion is visible on a hill to your left as you drive south from Redstone on State Route 82.

Along the Crystal River, adjacent to the highway going north from Redstone, are slabs and chunks of marble dropped from trains that once went to Carbondale. To learn more about that marble, read on.

When You Go

Redstone is 30 miles south of Glenwood Springs and 47 miles west of Aspen. Take State Route 133 south for 17 miles from the junction with State Route 82, near Carbondale.

Marble

"The Marble Capital of the United States" was initially settled by prospectors who formed a camp known as Yule Creek, named for pioneer George Yule. Gold, silver, and lead were mined from 1880 into the 1890s.

Even before the prospectors found their deposits, geologist Sylvester Richardson had noted in 1873 the beds of marble in Whitehouse Mountain. The marble was merely a curiosity then, because it was on the Ute Reservation.

After the Utes were moved west to allow prospectors in, attempts to quarry the stone in the 1880s enjoyed limited profitability because of the area's remoteness from a railhead. Even a quarry opened in the 1890s by the otherwise-successful John Cleveland Osgood of Redstone did not fare well.

The standard-gauge Crystal River & San Juan Railroad was completed from Carbondale in 1906, connecting the finishing mill at Marble with the Denver & Rio

Grande branch line to Aspen. That rail link, combined with a four-mile-long electric railway that transported marble from the quarry to the huge finishing mill, made production much more lucrative. The first large order, for a Cleveland courthouse, invigorated the community.

The best years followed, peaking from 1912 to 1917. The town was, literally, made by and of marble. Entire buildings were constructed of it, as were foundations and even sidewalks.

The town of Marble had its share of setbacks. A fire in 1916 destroyed much of downtown. Avalanches buried the finishing mill and the railroad tracks. Financial problems forced the closure of the quarry in 1941, as consumers began to order veneers instead of blocks or to

Left: *You will want to explore the ruins of the finishing mill, where blocks were cut, polished, and carved into everything from monuments to building blocks to tombstones.*

Above, top: *From the Marble Finishing Mill came the most prized marble in the United States. It was used for the Lincoln Memorial, the Washington Monument, and the Tomb of the Unknowns. For the latter, only the Yule Quarry could produce the fifty-six-ton slab required.*

Above, bottom: *Workers are dwarfed by the walls of marble inside the Yule Quarry in about 1910. (Courtesy of the Aspen Historical Society.)*

Crystal's hydroelectric generating plant was operational when this photo was taken in the 1890s. Note the dam across the Crystal River and, behind it, the large number of buildings standing in Crystal. (Courtesy of the Aspen Historical Society.)

choose cheaper marble substitutes. Mudslides in that year took large portions of the business section. Machinery, rails, even metal window frames were salvaged for scrap during World War II. Its glory days apparently over, Marble became a town of pleasant summer cabins.

When I first visited Marble in 1987, the Yule Quarry was still closed. We took a four-wheel-drive road there and stared at the piles of marble strewn along the old railroad bed. Near the entrance to the quarry itself was a mass of marble rubble that dwarfed us. Looking inside the quarry from two vantage points, we peered down into an alabaster monolithic city with sculptured walls and pillars sitting in a blue-green lagoon. Ropes, pulleys, and fragmented wooden ladders clung to the marble walls. It was mid-summer, yet the water had places where the sun had neglected it, and it was frozen—not universally frozen, but solid in the shapes of the surrounding marble cliffs, etched in straight lines and parallelograms.

The quarry reopened in the early 1990s and, unfortu-

nately, is closed to visitors at this writing.

West of the road to the quarry stands the town's major attraction, the ruins of the Marble Finishing Mill. Exploring this enchanting place is like wandering through an Indiana Jones adventure site—an ancient city with its marble pillars, brushy overgrowth, and occasional quarry blocks. One finished slab is a huge octagon about six and a half feet high that looks like a sacrificial stone from some primitive civilization.

Downtown Marble is quietly alive with a bed and breakfast inn, a museum (inside the old two-story high school, a wooden building with a marble foundation and marble columns on its porch), a general store, several residences, and galleries featuring marble sculptures. The museum is located on Main west of Third Street. There you will find information on a self-guided walking tour, which will direct you to the town's attractions.

One curious place nearby is at the southeast corner of Park and Third Streets (the only four-way stop in town).

It is an RV park with marble pieces standing in a bewildering assortment of shapes. It looks like a graveyard in which the headstones were carved by Salvador Dali.

East on Road 314 is the Marble Community Church, moved to Marble from Aspen in 1908. The Marble City State Bank Building is on Main near First Street, and beyond it are some attractive residences. One-half mile east of the four-way stop is a sign directing you to Crystal, but that route becomes four-wheel-drive-only within a mile.

You pass the Marble Cemetery on your way into town. It is on the north side of the road 2.2 miles west of the four-way stop. As you would expect, most markers are indeed made of marble. The largest stone is a particularly well-carved Woodmen of the World marker with five stacked logs; it is for John Franklin Clayton, who died in 1911.

When You Go
Marble is almost 11 miles from Redstone. Drive south 4.9 miles on State Route 133. Turn east on Road 314 and go 5.9 miles. Along the way, look for marble chunks that fell off rail cars over the years. At a spot only .3 of a mile from the outskirts of town, a veritable avalanche of marble sits among the aspens.

Crystal

The sign east of Marble indicates four-wheel-drive vehicles only to Crystal. Heed that warning. When I first saw Crystal, I was on a mountain bike, so I wasn't too concerned about the road. The next time, I was in my truck and glad to have a second driver with a four-wheel-drive vehicle ahead of me as we slipped and slogged our way to Crystal the day after a thunderstorm. Even in dry conditions the route would have been tricky. A pleasant alternative is to take a commercial tour of the Crystal area (inquire in Marble).

If you are a collector of books on Colorado, you will immediately recognize the first sign of Crystal—the remains of what is called the Crystal Mill, perched dramatically on a rocky crag.

Everyone says this structure is the Crystal Mill, but it really isn't. When Muriel Sibell Wolle made a drawing of the 1892 Sheep Mountain Tunnel Mill in 1947, her sketch showed a dilapidated mill standing next to this building. Caroline Bancroft has a photo from 1954 that shows the same mill in ruins. What remains is actually not the mill itself, but the hydroelectric power generator, last used in 1916, for the now-vanished mill.

The town of Crystal is .2 of a mile beyond the "mill."

The Crystal Club, made of stout logs except for a lumber false front, stands empty on the main street of Crystal.

One look at the clear river water running through the valley and you might surmise that this is how Crystal got its name. But you would be mistaken. It was not named for the water but rather for the silver-bearing quartz shot with crystallite that was found by prospectors in 1880.

Seven working silver mines kept Crystal going, and a road built over Schofield Pass to Gothic and Crested Butte (see chapter six) in 1883 helped get supplies in and ore out. A later road went to Carbondale via the route you take into town. By 1886, about four hundred people lived in the town that had two newspapers (including one using a wonderful pun, the *Crystal River Current*), two hotels, saloons, billiard parlor, barber shop, and the men-only Crystal Club.

The 1893 Silver Crash nearly emptied the town, and by 1915 only eight people lived there. A one-year mining venture brought the population up to seventy-five the next year, but after its failure, the town was deserted.

Crystal today contains about a dozen old cabins and the Crystal Club.

The road east from Crystal ascends Schofield Pass, which I have not attempted in a motorized vehicle, but I did ride on a mountain bike. On that occasion, the road was closed and a large snow field (in mid-July!) caused us to portage our bikes.

When You Go
Crystal is 5.9 miles east of downtown Marble on Road 314.

Chapter Six

CRESTED BUTTE GHOSTS

Left: *At an elevation of 11,605 feet, the Alpine Tunnel is the highest site featured in this book. The ruins of the engine house, which burned in 1906, stand in the re-creation of where a spur of track once stood. Restoration plans include rebuilding the arches at each end of the en-gine house, using the original stones that remain there.*

Above: *What more natural purchase could you make from the general store in Tincup than, well, a tin cup?*

Gunnison-area mining towns are delightfully varied, but all are located in magnificent scenery. The towns include Crested Butte, a popular skiing and mountain biking destination; Baldwin and Irwin, two nearly uninhabited sites; Gothic, a modern research center in a quaint old town; and Tincup, Pitkin, and Ohio City, three communities with photogenic buildings. The area also includes one of the most spectacular drives in Colorado, the old railroad route to the Alpine Tunnel.

Crested Butte

I admit it. I have lost all objectivity about Crested Butte. When I first rode a mountain bike into town, coming from Gunnison over Ohio Pass, I was completely captivated. Eleven years and seven visits later, the love affair continues. Crested Butte is my favorite Colorado town.

The place has energy and spirit, youth and amiability. What it lacks is pretension. Does it tell you something that arguably the best of the town's many fine restaurants is in a log cabin whose entrance fronts an alley?

That lack of pretension may come from the fact that Crested Butte was not a glory town. Its wealth came from coal, not gold or silver. As a result, this was a blue-collar town, where logs were fine, lumber was better, and fancy brick was nonexistent.

Crested Butte is the namesake of the mountain that dominates the eastern skyline. The town was settled in 1879 by prospectors looking for gold and silver, which they found near Gothic and Irwin. Crested Butte became a vital supply center for those mining camps, but even more so for the distant towns of Aspen and Ashcroft, which were booming, but isolated. Crested Butte had a railroad spur from Gunnison by 1881, so supplies could be freighted over Pearl Pass to those burgeoning silver towns until a railroad reached Aspen in 1887.

At the same time, Crested Butte's coal deposits, overlooked by the region's first prospectors, began to attract attention. The deposits were unusual in that both bituminous and anthracite coal were found within the same mines.

Coal provided life for Crested Butte. The Colorado Fuel and Iron Company owned the major mines around town, and a bank of 150 coke ovens stood south of

Behind the town of Crested Butte is Mount Crested Butte, a 12,162-foot peak so named by the Hayden Survey Party in 1874. Today the mountain provides excellent ski slopes for winter visitors.

town along a railroad spur.

Life in Crested Butte was not easy. Labor disputes were common, and underage boys did men's work. The cemetery north of town attests to the dangers of working at the Jokerville Mine. The winters were so severe that an architectural oddity was apparently born here: the two-story outhouse. The second story was used during the heavy winter snows when the lower floor was unreachable.

Coal mining died in the 1950s as the nationwide demand for coal plummeted. But investors, following Aspen's lead, purchased a nearby ranch and developed a ski resort at Mount Crested Butte, bringing the older town back to life. That resort is far enough away to assure the preservation of Crested Butte without destroying its character, although some longtime residents might disagree.

Walking and Driving Around Crested Butte

As you roam Crested Butte, be sure to look down alleys and back streets for old cabins and shacks, many of which now serve as outbuildings to the restored houses along the principal streets.

Elk Avenue is the main thoroughfare. Many clapboard false-front buildings line the street—some old, some simply old-looking. On Elk at Second Street is the 1883 former town hall and fire company, featuring a delicately arched cornice topped by a bell tower. Behind it on Second is the 1883 town jail.

Prospectors hoped to find placer gold like this small sample in their pans as they worked the streams of Colorado.

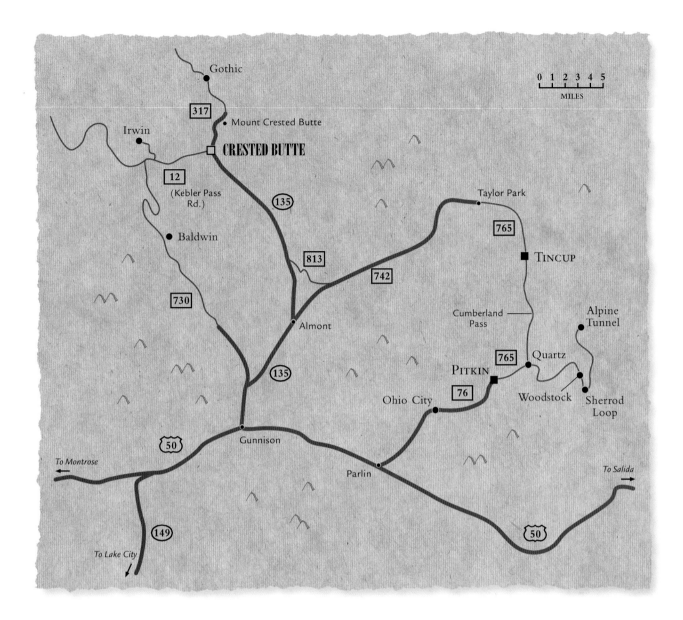

Across the street from the former town hall is the Forest Queen, built in the 1880s as a saloon and brothel. Next door is Kochevar's, a three-story hand-hewn timber building erected by taxidermist Jake Kochevar in the early 1900s.

The Mountain Heritage Museum is at Sopris and Second, south of the jail. Housed in an 1880s commercial building, the museum has portraits and biographies of local residents that help to personalize the town. In a back room is the Mountain Bike Hall of Fame, a must-see place for cyclists.

On Maroon Avenue (one block north of Elk) at Fourth Street is one of the town's best buildings, the 1882 Union Congregational Church. The bell tower, which was brought from Irwin, was added in 1917. The church has a lovely interior.

Beyond Maroon and Fifth is the 1883 Old Rock School, now a library. On the same property is the former high school, now the town hall, built in 1927.

The attractive 1881 train depot stands on the east end of town on Elk beyond Seventh Street.

The Crested Butte Cemetery is north of town on the road to the ski resort. A particularly touching grave is for "Our Babies," the Metzler twin sons who were born in 1890 and died on the same day in 1891 after living only nineteen months.

When You Go

Crested Butte is 28 miles north of Gunnison on State Route 135.

Right: *The Rozman House was one of Crested Butte's most revered landmarks. Originally a log cabin, it was gentrified with lumber siding and decorative trim in 1910 (note the date centered in the lattice work). The house was dismantled in 1998, to the dismay of many citizens, because it was deemed uninhabitable. By the time you visit Crested Butte, however, a replica should be standing on the original location north of the town cemetery.*

Below: *Crested Butte's cemetery includes headstones bearing the names of people of German, Italian, Slavic, and Irish descent. One section contains the remains of fifty-eight men who died in the Jokerville Mine Explosion of January 24, 1884. Mount Crested Butte stands in the background.*

84

Gothic

Gothic was named for Gothic Mountain, the peak directly west of town, which was in turn named for the elaborate spires and pinnacles along its eastern face. It was a prospector's paradise, but not a miner's. There were enough quartz-bearing streaks in the hills that anybody could find one; locating a vein that would actually produce paying ore was another matter.

Those streaks attracted prospectors in 1879, and by 1881 Gothic was considered Gunnison County's most important mining camp. It had a post office, newspaper, eight saloons, a dance hall, and a population of almost a thousand.

Gothic also had a reputation. When former-president Ulysses S. Grant was touring Colorado, he asked to be taken to a wild mining camp; he was whisked to Gothic. But the rowdy times didn't last long. Most of the ore was only on the surface, and Gothic died after a few short years.

The town's last resident was one-time saloonkeeper Garwood H. Judd, who lived in Gothic for almost half a century. He nailed a sign over the door of the old town hall where he lived proclaiming himself "The Man Who Stayed." In 1928, a motion picture company came to Gothic and did a two-reel film about him.

In that same year, Dr. John C. Johnson of Western State College in Gunnison saw Gothic as a natural place to study high-elevation flora and fauna. He bought the seventy-acre town for two hundred dollars in back taxes and began instituting summer workshops that continue to this day as the Rocky Mountain Biological Laboratory. Early students attending workshops would visit with Garwood Judd, who would reminisce about life in the old mining camp while perusing a well-worn scrapbook. When Judd died in 1930, his ashes were scattered over the town, so he remains "The Man Who Stayed."

The Gothic townsite today features Garwood's old home, the two-story town hall, which dates from about 1880. At least two cabins are contemporaries of the town hall; several others were erected in the 1930s by the biological laboratory.

When You Go

Gothic is 7.5 miles north of Crested Butte. The paved road north from Crested Butte to Mount Crested Butte is County Road 317. (In Mount Crested Butte, Road 317 is Gothic Road.) Follow it through the ski resort. Keep on Road 317 when it turns to dirt and follow it to Gothic, 3.8 miles beyond the end of the pavement.

Gothic's town hall is now the visitors' center for the Rocky Mountain Biological Laboratory. There you can learn more about the laboratory's current projects and purchase refreshments and souvenirs.

Irwin

When ruby silver, a silver-arsenic sulfide mineral, was discovered in 1879 along what prospectors appropriately called Ruby Gulch, two communities came to life—Ruby and Irwin. The latter was named for Canadian prospector Richard Irwin, one of the first arrivals. When the towns were laid out, they were actually on Ute Reservation land. Reservation boundaries were soon altered to allow for miners, and the towns became part of Gunnison County. Irwin eventually absorbed Ruby.

When the town was only a year old, Irwin could boast of having the county's only brass band. According to the *Gunnison Review*, "the sweet music discoursed by it every evening has a charming effect, echoing through the gulches and over the distant hills and peaks."

Irwin ultimately had a main street with a row of two-story clapboard, false-front businesses and an elaborate

This empty house at Baldwin is one of only ten at the site. All are included in an area for sale as part of a development.

string of fire plugs to protect them. But the ore gave out quickly, and by 1885 the town was nearly deserted.

No original buildings stand in Irwin today. On an eastern hill are the headframe and other remnants of the Forest Queen Mine.

The Irwin Cemetery, originally the Ruby Cemetery, is located at Kebler Pass, which is .7 of a mile beyond the turnoff to Lake Irwin on Kebler Pass Road. The first inhabitant of about fifty in the cemetery supposedly died while using dynamite to kill fish. At that cemetery today, the only old headstone is for Mary Bambrough, who died in 1881 at age seventeen.

When You Go

Irwin is 6.9 miles west of Crested Butte. Take Kebler Pass Road (National Forest and Gunnison County Road 12) from Crested Butte 6.1 miles to the Lake Irwin turn-

off. Turn right toward Lake Irwin Campground, then take the first right (a high-clearance road heading north) for .8 of a mile to Irwin, passing through the Ruby townsite on the way.

Baldwin

Baldwin was a coal-mining town. Actually, it was two separate towns, one dating from 1881, the other from 1897. The mines were plagued by strikes that pitted non-union against union and labor against management. Dozens of men were killed during these disputes over the years, until the dropping demand for coal in the 1940s ended the mining and, consequently, the strife.

Today Baldwin is closed to the public and has signs warning against trespassing. The site consists of ten log buildings, only three under roof, all visible from the road.

When You Go

From downtown Gunnison, drive 3.4 miles north on State Route 135. Turn left onto Road 730, which goes over Ohio Pass. (Do not take Castle Mountain Road, which heads west.) Baldwin is 14.2 miles north.

From Irwin, take Forest Service Road 730 over Ohio Pass, which forks from Kebler Pass Road just below the Irwin cemetery, for 8.8 miles to Baldwin.

Tincup

Tincup is a charming log cabin town in a lovely setting. Some cabins are occupied by the descendants of early miners who stayed long after the ore gave out, simply because they loved Tincup. You will see why.

Tincup was probably named in 1860 when prospector Jim Taylor stopped for a drink and dipped into a cold mountain steam with his tin cup. In the water he saw gold flakes.

Gold mining was not pursued in earnest, however, until 1879 with the opening of the Gold Cup Mine. A post office was granted as Virginia, but within a year it was changed to Tin Cup. (The U.S. Postal Service, as it did to Fairplay and Redcliff, later made the name one word.)

Tincup was truly a lawless place. Of its first eight marshals, only one finished his term. The others quit, were fired, were shot, or went insane.

Eventually the town settled down, but the ore ran out in 1884. A minor rebirth occurred in the 1890s, when Tincup went modern with fire hydrants and telephones, and again in 1903, when the Brunswick Milling and Mining Company reworked old mines.

Despite the fire hydrants, the town's main business section burned in 1906 and again in 1913. In that same era, dredging operations along Willow Creek kept the town going, but the closing of the venerable Gold Cup Mine in 1917 ended large-scale mining.

Today, Tincup has a wonderful rustic charm. At least two dozen historic buildings, most of them log cabins and framed residences, are mixed with newer cabins, but the newer ones fit right in.

The Tincup Store is a natural place to stop. There you can purchase an obligatory tin cup or, more importantly, "A Place History of Tincup," which has an excellent guide map.

The town's most elaborate building is the 1903 town hall, still very much in use for Friday "family night" square dances and for Sunday worship.

Another attractive building east of the town hall is the Headley-Bley–La June House, a log home that features a

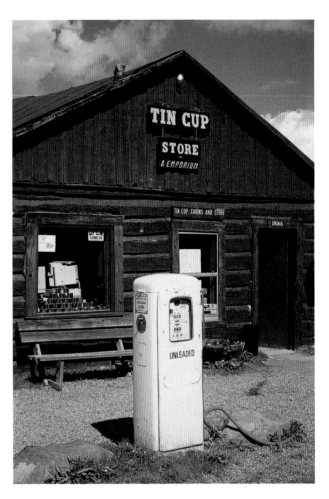

The Tincup Store was originally the headquarters for Forest Service Ranger William Kreutzer, who came to Tincup in 1905.

Tincup's town hall has an attractive, off-center steeple. Inside, simple benches and straight-back chairs provide the seating, while an organ and a piano provide the music.

Cumberland Pass and the Bon Ton Mine

Under normal weather conditions, the Cumberland Pass, which connects Tincup and Quartz, is one of the better unpaved high-mountain roads in Colorado. You will pass the waste dump and abandoned cabin of the Blistered Horn Mine, remnants of other cabins, and, eight miles from Tincup, the stunning views at Cumberland Pass. Looking north, you will have before you the craggy peaks of the Elk Mountains near Aspen.

Beyond Cumberland Pass 2.9 miles are the ruins of the Bon Ton Mine. The site has ruins of three log cabins, a hopper, and waste dumps on your left and about a half dozen remnants of cabins on your right.

Ruins of a log cabin frame the scant remnants of the Bon Ton Mine, which yielded gold, silver, copper, lead, and zinc.

clapboard false front with decorative wood trim.

The Tincup cemeteries are outside of town. To reach them, take Road 765 south. Just before it begins to ascend and curve to the right, turn left on a side road. Go right at the first fork (Road 765-2A) and left at the second. The cemeteries are .4 of a mile from Road 765.

Located on a series of knolls, four separate graveyards are connected by paths, catwalks, and bridges. The cemeteries are situated in a place of incredible beauty, with pine trees, Willow Creek, and a view of nearby Mount Kreutzer, named for pioneer ranger William Kreutzer.

The first knoll is the Jewish cemetery, which has one grave and perhaps a second. A footbridge leads across East Willow Creek to the Catholic Knoll, a small cemetery with many graves marked by simple wooden crosses. Another footbridge takes you west to the Protestant Knoll, by far the largest cemetery. Many older graves have newer wooden markers, and several graves date from recent times.

Boot Hill is the second-largest cemetery. It is a mostly untended graveyard beyond the Catholic Knoll to the east. Many graves are marked only by rock rectangles.

When You Go

Tincup is almost 40 miles from Gunnison via the town of Taylor Park. Take State Route 135 north from Gunnison. At Almont, 10 miles from Gunnison, take the right fork, Road 742, to Taylor Park. From there, take Road 765 another 7.3 miles to Tincup.

Along the way, about 2.5 miles before you reach the town, you will see extensive dredge tailings along Willow Creek.

If you are coming from Crested Butte, head south toward Gunnison on State Route 135. After almost 11 miles from Crested Butte, take the cutoff at Jacks Cabin (Road 813), which joins Road 742 to Taylor Park. Then follow the directions above.

From Tincup, you can continue south to visit the remaining sites listed in this chapter via the Cumberland Pass (see sidebar).

Quartz

Quartz was a silver mining camp in 1879 and 1880. When the railroad arrived in 1882, Quartz also served as a freight depot, where cargo was transferred from trains to wagons heading over Cumberland Pass.

Although nothing remains at the townsite today, at one time Quartz had two stores, several saloons, the Gunnison Ore Sampling Works, and about two hundred people. The railroad also had a section house, coal house, and telegraph office along a spur almost a half mile long.

Woodstock, Sherrod Loop, and the Alpine Tunnel

For one of the most unforgettable drives of your life, take the road heading east on the old railroad grade for 9.5 miles to the west portal of the Alpine Tunnel. I recommend driving a high-clearance vehicle on this road, although I saw several passenger cars negotiating the route. The road starts innocently enough, climbing through verdant forests. In 3.2 miles you will pass the base of an old water tank and, in another 3.2 miles, the Tunnel Gulch Tank.

Beyond the Tunnel Gulch Tank .7 of a mile is the site of Woodstock, a silver camp founded in 1881. The town was buried by an avalanche in March 1884; thirteen people were killed, including all six of Marcella Doyle's children. The town was never rebuilt.

Beyond Woodstock .4 of a mile is Sherrod Loop, the name of both a railroad loop and a later mining town that came to life in 1903. Named for W. H. Sherrod, a mining engineer, the town had a depot and a rail spur for shipment of local ore. It was a ghost town by 1906.

Sherrod Loop now has only the base of a solitary log cabin, but the town once boasted a hardware store, saloon, newspaper, and two hotels. The present road doesn't follow the loop, but you can see it go out and gracefully arch back to the place where the current road rejoins the old roadbed.

In the next 2.1 miles from Sherrod Loop, the route becomes absolutely spectacular. It traverses some of the most difficult terrain—and some of the most dramatically scenic—that an American railroad ever attempted to conquer. The route goes through potential rock slides, across the faces of mountains, and past an incredible wall built by skilled masons using mortarless, hand-cut fitted stones to hold the roadbed. The wall is 452 feet long, 33 feet high, and 2 feet thick. In more than a hundred years, very few stones have needed replacement.

One passenger on the railroad, coming through this area known as the Palisades, commented as he gawked through his downslope window, "There is scarcely three feet between one and eternity."

Beyond the Palisades is a parking lot for the Alpine Tunnel. The tunnel was constructed for the Denver, South Park & Pacific Railroad in 1881 and 1882 to connect Denver and Gunnison. The line went through St. Elmo, Romley, and the east portal town of Hancock (all discussed in chapter seven).

At the tunnel today, an 1883 telegraph office serves as the visitors' center. Nearby are the stone ruins of the engine house. An interpretive sign says that the tunnel itself is 1,771 feet long and took eighteen months to build, with a steady crew of 350 to 400 men. Turnover rates were high, due to the arduous construction and often impossible working conditions, along with the lure of riches in nearby mines. In the winter, crews had to travel from their cabins to the tunnel in groups to avoid getting disoriented and lost in the snow.

At this writing, both this portal and the east one near Hancock are covered with debris. Restoration efforts are planned so that visitors will eventually be able to see into the tunnel itself and perhaps even to walk in a few feet.

When you return from the portal to the telegraph office, look more closely at the engine house. You can see where the turntable and water tank were housed in this immense structure.

The Alpine Tunnel was abandoned in 1910 due to a lack of freight business. One water tank was dismantled and moved to an active line between Como and Breckenridge. It is now called Baker Tank (see page 55). Tom Clauter, who volunteers at the visitors' center, joked that he and his friends would love to sneak over one night and return Baker Tank to its original location. When you view that tank, you will see how simple a project that would be.

Above: *The only remaining water tank along the route between the Quartz townsite and the Alpine Tunnel is Tunnel Gulch Tank, which was restored in 1969. Tanks of this type could fill a train's tender in less than five minutes at three hundred to four hundred gallons per minute.*

On that spur was the town's most unusual feature—a jail on wheels, made from two converted box cars.

When You Go

To get to Quartz, follow the Cumberland Pass past the Bon Ton Mine (see sidebar). Quartz is 5.1 miles beyond the Bon Ton.

Pitkin

Pitkin was founded in 1879, a year after the first claims were filed near Fairview Peak. The first post office was for Quartzville, but the name was changed after only a few months to honor Frederick W. Pitkin, the state's second governor, who was in office at the time. The tent community evolved into a log cabin town as the price of lots skyrocketed from five dollars each to more than seven hundred dollars as prospectors found silver and gold along the Quartz Creek Valley.

A major problem was getting ore to market, and many miners went bankrupt with stockpiled ore they could not ship. That problem was solved in 1882 when the Denver, South Park & Pacific Railroad reached Pitkin through the Alpine Tunnel. That was Pitkin's best year, and the town reached its peak population of about twenty-five hundred. (One negative of the railroad was that its construction crews were decidedly more rough than Pitkin's citizens. When they came to town, people locked their doors and went to bed. When the railroad crews worked toward Gunnison, normality returned.)

When silver was demonetized by the Sherman Act in 1893, the gold claims became vital to Pitkin's existence. They lasted until about 1916. After that, Pitkin had a less dramatic second life as a timber town. By the 1970s, the population was down to a couple of dozen. The excellent weather, however, has brought many people back to Pitkin for the summers, when the population swells to about two hundred.

Today new cabins and larger houses stretch for blocks, but they don't detract from the town's historic elements. If you are coming from the north, the street that heads south is State Street, the former railroad bed. A handsome depot stands at State and Sixth.

Other attractive buildings are one block west on Main Street. In addition to several old residences, you will find the Pitkin Community Church (ca. 1900), the post office, and Pitkin Trading Company General Merchandise. Of special note are the Pitkin Hotel in the 1904 Mason Block and the 1900 city hall, restored in 1997 by the Colorado Historical Society. The city hall has an attractive stained-glass window on the second floor, which is reached by climbing the two sets of covered stairs outside of the building.

Farther south on the west side of Main Street are the considerable stone foundations of a mill behind the Quartz Creek Lodge.

To visit the Pitkin Cemetery, turn west on the road south of the lodge. The right fork is Cemetery Road. A thoughtful touch at this cemetery is a series of copper-colored markers that give interesting biographical information about people for whom there are no stones. The largest marker is of pot metal, the kind often ordered through a catalogue, for Edith Vivian Dickinson, who died in 1902. One elegantly simple epitaph is for Dr. A. F. Pettengill; it reads, "He went about doing good."

When You Go

Pitkin is 2.5 miles south of the site of Quartz on Road 765.

Ohio City

Gold was found in the 1860s in nearby Ohio Creek, but it wasn't until 1879 that a silver rush brought prospectors to Quartz Creek. The settlement that formed at the confluence of Quartz and Ohio Creeks was originally called Eagle City. When a post office was granted in 1880, it was for Ohio, after the creek that had been named by prospectors from that state. The creek later was called Gold Creek after placer gold was found there. Although the U.S. Postal Service and maps call the town Ohio, residents prefer Ohio City.

The 1880s were good times for Ohio City. Chicago financiers backed many enterprises, including the Chicago Mine, a hotel, and other buildings. They also influenced a place name—the cemetery sits near Illinois Gulch.

The 1893 Silver Crash dealt the town a blow, but production continued in area gold mines on a decreasing basis until World War II, when mining of non-strategic minerals was prohibited.

The most photogenic structure in Ohio City is the city hall. Southeast of that building are some interesting log cabins at Roller and Gunnison Streets.

A large log cabin with a sod roof stands west of town. Drive .7 of a mile from the city hall (on your way you will see the cemetery on a hill to your right, but there is no road to it) and turn right on Road 882. The cabin is .5 of a mile up that road.

When You Go

Ohio City is 6.3 miles south of Pitkin on Gunnison County Road 76, which is the name of Road 765 when it becomes paved on the north end of Pitkin.

Above: *Originally known as the Bon Ton Hotel, the Pitkin Hotel (motto: "A Step Back in Time") is at this writing a hostel offering inexpensive accommodations. It is also being restored by the Colorado Historical Society with monies from the Colorado Historical Fund.*

Right: *The 1906 Ohio City Hall is a classic false-front building, with pressed-tin siding and a front door jauntily set on the diagonal.*

Chapter Seven

St. Elmo Ghosts

Left: *Now-peaceful St. Elmo once exploded with activity as a mining center and a Saturday-night town.*

Above: *Doc Courtwright looked out of this window from his home in Bonanza. Doc was technically a veterinarian, but he did human doctoring as well.*

The majority of the sites listed in this chapter are true ghost towns—at this writing, five are empty. Unfortunately, all except one are rather empty of buildings as well. That exception is Turret, which has an abandoned look to entice your camera or sketchpad. St. Elmo, the chapter's principal attraction, has one of the most photogenic main streets in the West.

St. Elmo

St. Elmo resembles what many people picture when someone mentions a "ghost town." With its gorgeous scenery and attractive buildings, it is one of Colorado's premier "ghost" destinations.

The Heightly Cottage (left) and the two-story combination Comfort Hotel and Stark Brothers Store are attached in an architecturally creative way. The store also housed the post office, telephone exchange, and telegraph.

Originally, the townsite that grew along Chalk Creek in 1879 was aptly called Forest City for the numerous spruce and pine trees in the area. But the Postal Service refused the name, because a Forest City already existed in California. A committee of three chose the name St. Elmo (the patron saint of sailors) because of a popular 1866 novel of that name.

Silver and gold strikes in the Chalk Creek Mining District early in 1880 brought hundreds to St. Elmo, which became a supply center for nearby mines and a jumping off point for prospectors heading over passes to boom towns such as Tincup and Aspen.

When the Denver, South Park & Pacific Railroad was completed to St. Elmo, the town's future seemed assured. It became a favorite place for miners, freighters, and railroad workers to spend their Saturday nights, as they enjoyed St. Elmo's many saloons.

Because of the travel trade, the town had five hotels. One guest, upon arriving at a hotel still getting its finishing touches, asked for a private room. The hotelier drew a chalk line around one of many beds and told him that he had even given him a suite.

The failure of one mine after another and the closing of the Alpine Tunnel in 1910 began the decline of St. Elmo. The Stark family, who owned the first house in town, remained after all others left. Muriel Sibell Wolle fondly recalls Mr.

Silver ore may be less spectacular in appearance than gold, but it was primarily silver that fueled Colorado's early prosperity.

Stark in her book *Stampede to Timberline.* She said he was very gracious, insisting upon bringing her an armchair while she sketched. When she left his store in the otherwise empty town, he warned, "Watch out for the streetcars!" She does not identify him except as Mr. Stark, but it was brothers Roy and Tony, along with their sister Annabelle, who ran the store until the late 1950s. After Wolle's book came out, the Starks criticized her for daring to call St. Elmo a ghost town and blamed her for their lack of business.

St. Elmo today has more than forty antique structures. As you enter town, you will pass two restored buildings, the Pawnee Mill's livery stable and its blacksmith shop. A house across the street is an information center for the Colorado Historical Society.

The current center of activity is the Miners Exchange, a log building with a frame false front, where you can purchase all manner of ghost town and Colorado merchandise. Perhaps the most enjoyable item to buy is food for the insatiable chipmunks that cadge snacks from visitors.

The other buildings, although closed to visitors at this writing, are clearly visible from the street. They include the town hall and jail, with its belfry for fire alarms and its combination telephone booth and fire tool storage locker. Across the street is the Stark Brothers Store and sixteen-bedroom Home Comfort Hotel, built around

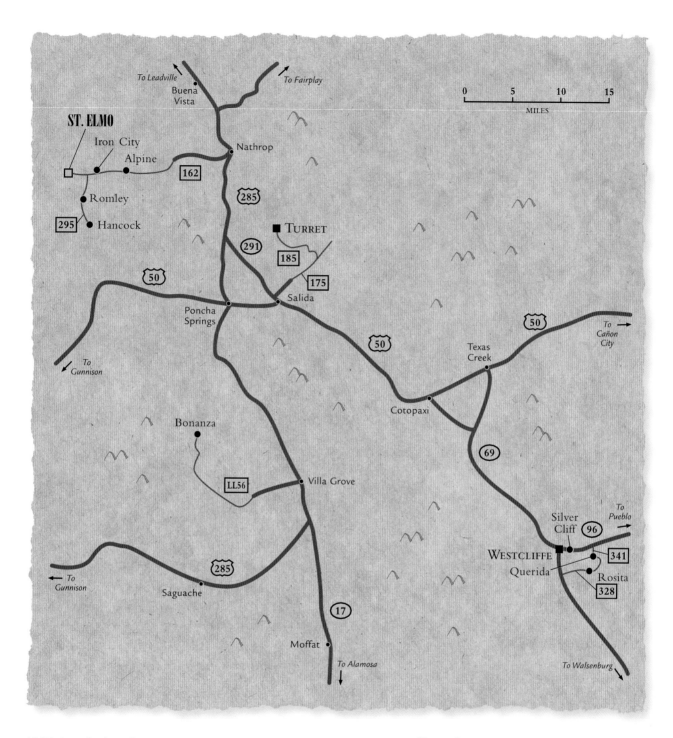

1885. Attached to the Stark store is the 1881 Heightley Cottage.

The road to Tincup Pass heads north from town. Take that road to see the 1882 one-room school, then follow the road as it turns west to view two stores and several residences.

When You Go

St. Elmo is 24 miles southwest of Buena Vista and 33 miles northwest of Salida via U.S. 285. Take U.S. 285 to Nathrop; just .3 of a mile south of Nathrop is Road 162. Take this road 15.4 miles west to St. Elmo.

Romley and Hancock

Romley

All that remains of Romley are heaps of rubble that contain items such as pressed tin, bed springs, and log beams.

Romley was the town nearest the Mary Murphy Mine, discovered in the 1870s and, according to lore, named for a woman who nursed a hospitalized miner to health. The Mary Murphy was the principal mine in the Chalk Creek District, yielding more than $14 million in ore by 1917. Worked intermittently after that, it closed for good during World War II.

Beyond Romley 1.7 miles is the large ore-sorting house and bin of the Alley Belle Mine. When the legs of the bin failed, the bin tipped down and the sorting house settled on top of it, resulting in this precarious lean out over the former railroad right-of-way, now the road to Hancock.

Beyond the Romley townsite is a four-wheel-drive road to the Mary Murphy, .8 of a mile southeast, where a half-dozen buildings stand. The largest, a wood-frame structure with a pressed-tin facade, might have been a dormitory or company office.

Hancock

Although Hancock had been a mining camp for several years, its most prosperous times began in 1881 when it became the temporary camp for construction crews working on the Alpine Tunnel, the first railroad tunnel to pass under the Continental Divide (see chapter six). Five stores, a hotel, saloons, restaurants, and two sawmills served the community of about five hundred. When the tunnel was completed, a population of about two hundred remained. But when the tunnel route was eliminated in 1910, Hancock was doomed.

Hancock's only remnant is the log foundation of a saloon. The east portal of the Alpine Tunnel is about 3.5 miles away, and a hiking and equestrian trail to the portal begins beyond the town. (Note: You can also visit the tunnel's west portal. See chapter six.)

When You Go

Romley is 2.6 miles up Road 295, which heads south from Road 162, the route to St. Elmo. Road 162 begins .3 of a mile east of St. Elmo. Hancock is 2.6 miles beyond Romley. Although I would recommend a truck for this road, a passenger sedan was parked at Hancock, making me feel less intrepid than I wanted to.

Iron City

Iron City, a smelter town that lived for only two years, has disappeared, but its cemetery remains, used long after the town was dead. There are eighty-some graves, with an interesting touch added by June Sheputts, who in 1992 posted a list of names with cause of death, when known, of those interred. Those causes include "mine accident,"

Once a hotel early in Turret's history, this log building (with a later frame addition) has since served as a shelter for livestock.

"apoplexy," "starved and froze," "powder explosion," "burned in house," "typhoid," "old army wound," "pneumonia," "diphtheria," "miner's consumption," "suicide," "snow slide," and "murdered by husband." That list is a testament to the hard life of the mining town.

One of the most memorable epitaphs I have ever read was for Sarah and Sadie Mullins: "Born a year apart, died a day apart, buried a hand apart."

When You Go

From downtown St. Elmo, return east on Road 162 for .1 of a mile. Turn north onto Road 292 and follow it .7 of a mile through a campground.

Alpine

Although I could see not one building of antiquity in Alpine, a town founded in 1877, I did find an interesting cemetery there. About a dozen marked graves, including a couple of wooden markers, and an indeterminate num-

ber of unmarked graves make up the site.

When You Go

To reach the Alpine Cemetery from St. Elmo, go east on Road 162, the road back to U.S. 285, for 3.5 miles to Alpine. Make a right turn after the bridge, and turn left .2 of a mile later onto Road 292. Go straight through the next intersection and turn right on the next road, which has a "Dead End" sign. (Well, it *is* going to a cemetery.) Park at the end and walk north about thirty yards to see the first stones.

Turret

Turret was the destination for a minor rush in 1897 when the Gold Bug and Vivandiere claims were filed. Tents and then cabins lined a street along Cat Gulch within weeks. The town, named for nearby Turret Mountain, had a post office the following year. A 1902 photograph shows a main street with at least a dozen log and frame buildings, including the two-story Gregory Hotel. At that time the population was estimated at five hundred.

Turret miner and saloonkeeper Emil Becker had been a major-league baseball player. One of his old teammates, evangelist Billy Sunday, came to visit Becker in Turret, and for that one day, Becker was only a miner, having closed his saloon out of deference to Sunday's strong temperance stance.

Most of the area mines played out almost immediately. The town's biggest producer, the Independence, was worked sporadically until 1916.

When Muriel Sibell Wolle visited Turret in 1941, she saw a ghost town with only one summer resident. When author/historian Caroline Bancroft was there in 1960, she counted fifteen houses, one of which, she said, might have been the Gregory Hotel. When author Norman Weis wrote of his trip to Turret in the 1970s, he was with a Salida resident who identified practically every building in town, including the post office, city hall, saloon, brothel, and the Gregory Hotel. On my visit in 1997 I found most of the buildings Weis described, although time—

Little more than a skeleton remains of Robinson's General Store in Turret.

and vandals, no doubt—had certainly worn down the town.

Turret has three separate sections. No buildings were occupied when I was there, although there was evidence of recent habitation.

In the western section, where a side road ends at a turnaround, stand ten buildings, including a four-room cabin. Another is a three-room cabin that has a cistern out front. A one-room cabin behind it had the luxury of a fence—the posts and gate still stand.

East of this area is the center section of town, which features five more buildings. The largest is a two-story frame structure covered with ornamental tin. This was the town hall during Turret's heyday but was later converted to a residence.

Robinson's General Store, a long wooden structure standing beside the main road, once sold "everything from dynamite to needles to canned goods," according to Salida resident Tommi Holden. Behind it is a two-story hewn-

log building that was one of the town's first hotels. The better known Gregory Hotel was, unfortunately, dismantled and sold for lumber salvage in about 1984.

East of this area along the main road stand five more dilapidated cabins, one with a partial sod roof. Beyond them is one modern cabin posted against trespassing. Beyond that, at a turnaround, is a hewn-log cabin that appears quite habitable.

When You Go

Turret is 12 miles north of Salida. Take State Route 291 northwest. One mile from downtown, turn north on Road 175 at the sign for Spiral Drive. Cross the Arkansas River and then take the next right, Road 175, which you will follow for 6.7 miles. At the junction of Roads 175 and 185, at a quarry in Railroad Gulch, turn west (left) and follow the main road for the next 4.2 miles. All but the last two miles are easy driving suitable for any vehicle.

Bonanza

The first evidence that you are entering ghost town country will begin almost thirteen miles up the road from Villa Grove to Bonanza, when you will come to the sparse remnants of Sedgwick, a suburb of Bonanza. The town was plotted in July 1880 and had a population of 650 within five months. All that remained when I visited were piles of boards.

Beyond Sedgwick .4 of a mile, where the road crosses Kerber Creek, was Kerber City, a second "suburb" to Bonanza. Only ruins of the Little Bonanza Mill west of the creek mark this site.

Bonanza begins one mile beyond Kerber City with the ruins of the Bonanza Mill and one tin-covered wood building. There are about half a dozen old structures in town along with a few newer residences.

Bonanza was founded in 1880 when prospectors fanned out from Leadville searching for the next strike. The area's first mine was the Exchequer, followed by the Bonanza, so named because its discoverer shouted, "Boys, she's a bonanza!" People flocked to the community named for the mine and to the nearby town of Exchequerville (later Exchequer). Bonanza, which became the largest of the four towns, had seven dance halls, thirty-six saloons, and a population of about fifteen hundred.

The ore, however, turned out to be of rather low quality, and Bonanza shortly emptied. But new technology in the milling process brought the place back to a modest, non-bonanza life. By 1899, the town was down to about a hundred citizens. The Rawley Mine turned out to be the best producer; when it finally shut down in the 1930s, it had delivered $6 million in lead and silver.

Most of the activity in Bonanza today involves environmental clean up, which began in 1994 with the removal of tailings at the Rawley Mill. A sign in town tells local history and has a map of four-wheel-drive loops in the area. A city map shows where various buildings once stood, including the school, town hall, bank, doctor's office, saloons, and hotels.

One mile north of Bonanza is Exchequer, where a cabin and a horse corral stand. Southeast of the townsite is the Exchequer Cemetery.

Buried here, among at least two dozen graves, is a woman who wrote a Western American classic. Anne Ellis (1875–1938) was convinced by two friends to write of her experiences in Bonanza and other mining towns. The

result, *The Life of an Ordinary Woman*, shows she was not ordinary in anyone's eyes but her own. Her travails and her observations about life make hers one of the best books about the pioneer West. Here is a wry example from her life, in which she reveals a desire, in her very early years, to end it all:

Once, when things had gone worse than usual, I decided to commit suicide, my plan being to crawl into a big snowdrift, and die there. I thought how sorry they would feel in the spring when the snow went off, and I was found. I hoped I would not look like a cat we had found early one April!—but—Mama had just made two custard pies, the frosting sweating huge drops of gold, and had put them on the cupboard shelf to cool. So I put off the dreadful act til they were eaten, and always since then, there has been something, if not a pie to save me.

Buried near Anne Ellis are her mother Rachel, her brother Edward, and her half-brother Will. Her mother's headstone revealed a discrepancy I cannot explain. In her book, Ellis says her mother's last name was "Levon," not "Leavitt," as is on her stone.

There is a Bonanza Cemetery as well. As you leave Bonanza and head toward Villa Grove on Road LL56, turn left on a road obliquely heading up a hill opposite tailings on your right. At least two dozen graves seem to be in the cemetery, although numbers are somewhat difficult to estimate. One marker is for Homer M. Booth, born in Westford, Vermont, who died in 1881, early in the "bonanza," at age twenty-four.

The Bonanza Mine's Cucamonga Mill was covered with asphalt sheeting, no doubt as inexpensive insulation. The mill and headframe stand north of the site of Exchequer.

On your return trip, about four miles before the highway, you will top a rise and have an astonishing view of the western face of the Sangre de Cristo Mountains. I saw this panorama with the late afternoon sun reddening the landscape. Perhaps it was a similar view that caused the Spaniards to name these mountains for the "Blood of Christ."

When You Go

Bonanza is 14.5 miles northwest of Villa Grove and 40 miles southwest of Salida. Take Road LL56, which begins .2 of a mile north of Villa Grove.

Moffat

Moffat, a small community in the San Luis Valley, technically doesn't belong in this book since it is neither a ghost town nor was it a mining camp. But it has four quite appealing buildings and is less than twenty minutes south of Villa Grove, so I thought it was worth including.

Moffat was a railroad town named for David H. Moffat, president of the Denver & Rio Grande Railroad, who constructed a line from Villa Grove south to Alamosa. The current highway, State Route 17, follows that route. (Incidentally, also named for David Moffat is Moffat County, in Colorado's northwest corner, and the Moffat Tunnel, familiar to skiers traveling by train between Denver and Winter Park.)

Moffat's historic structures are east of the highway. The most obvious is a church that appears to have been the First Baptist, but the denomination has been obliterated, even on the cornerstone, which was laid on August 6, 1911.

The most imposing building is a two-story brick residence on the corner of Moffat Way and Broadway. Just west of that house are the wood-frame town hall and the tin-faced, false-front former Bank of Moffat.

When You Go

Moffat is 18 miles south of Villa Grove on State Route 17.

Westcliffe, Silver Cliff, Querida, and Rosita

Westcliffe

Westcliffe is the primary town of interest in this area, but a pleasant back-roads loop takes you to three lesser sites, each of which was a booming silver town that flashed brightly but faded quickly. Westcliffe endured because it had something more permanent than mineral wealth.

Westcliffe came to life with the arrival of the Denver

Above: *The deserted town hall in Moffat is an excellent example of an unadorned, lumber-milled, false-front building. Since town halls usually did not occupy false fronts (as they had no reason to advertise), this building probably served a commercial purpose originally.*

Facing page: *Silver Cliff has been overtaken by Westcliffe, its one-time smaller neighbor. As a result, Silver Cliff has more of a "ghost town" look, such as these leaning and toppled outbuildings.*

& Rio Grande Railroad in 1881, which was extended to the area to serve the mines of Silver Cliff. A story claims that Dr. William A. Bell, a friend of the railroad's president, named the town for his birthplace in England, Westcliffe-on-the-Sea. Bell, however, was born in County Tipperary, Ireland. In reality, the town was probably called Westcliffe because it was west of "Cliff," the common nickname of Silver Cliff.

It was the smaller neighbor to Silver Cliff until the 1893 Silver Crash, when Silver Cliff began to die. Westcliffe, however, had the railroad and so lived on.

Westcliffe today is a picturesque town with some attractive buildings scattered throughout the community. For example, the downtown features a large feed store at Second and North, a former bank on the northeast corner of Second and Main, and the utilitarian stone block

Jennings Market across from the bank. The former railroad depot is hard to recognize. Now a residence, it is partially hidden by trees west of Second on the south side of Main.

A short driving tour will take you past several other architecturally interesting structures. At the corner of Second and Rosita, one block south of Main, stands the W. Wolff Block, which features an attractive stone front.

Continue south on Second and you will soon see the tall spire of the 1917 Lutheran church. East of the church stands the beautiful 1891 Westcliffe School.

On the southwest corner of Seventh and Main is an 1880s hewn-log house that was disassembled and moved to town, where local craftsman Ed Thornton painstakingly restored it in 1995.

Silver Cliff

Silver Cliff is a mile east of Westcliffe on State Route 9. In 1878, horn silver was discovered on a cliff thirty feet high, thereby giving a name to the town that developed nearby. A three-year bonanza brought five thousand people to Silver Cliff, making it Colorado's third-largest city at the time.

In 1881, the same year the railroad created Westcliffe, the town was almost completely destroyed by fire, despite the efforts of two fire companies.

In 1886, Silver Cliff, with votes from Westcliffe assisting, took the county seat from Rosita. Angry residents there refused to give up the records, so vigilantes went to Rosita and seized them. In recognition of Westcliffe's help in securing the county seat, the courthouse was built halfway between the two towns.

The Silver Crash of 1893 closed Silver Cliff's mines, and by 1900 the population had plummeted to less than six hundred. A decade later, it was less than three hundred. Many of the town's buildings were moved, most to Westcliffe. In 1928, when there was little else to plunder, Westcliffe took the county seat and built itself a new courthouse.

Today Silver Cliff looks rather dowdy compared to Westcliffe. The 1879 town hall and fire station, located at Main and Fleetwood, later became a museum. It was closed when I visited and appeared permanently closed. At the corner of Main and Mill stands an old brick store that has been remodeled. At First and Fleetwood is the 1888 Casebeer House, and west of it is the 1878 Silver Cliff School, now a residence.

To visit the town's two cemeteries, drive south on Mill for almost a mile from Main. The Silver Cliff Cemetery is situated on an expansive plain, affording a good view of the northern hills that had Silver Cliff's mines and a magnificent view southwest of the Sangre de Cristo Mountains. A half-mile southeast is the smaller Assumption Catholic Cemetery.

Querida

Querida is southeast of Silver Cliff. Drive east on State Route 96 for 6.2 miles to Road 341 and turn south. In one mile you will come to some tailings dumps and a pond, a couple of vacant buildings, and, finally, a stone block retaining wall near a modern power transformer. This mortarless wall is all that remains of the Bassick Mine and Mill, and what you just passed was Querida.

Querida existed because of the Bassick Mine. Edmund Bassick, who had made and lost fortunes in both the California and Australian gold rushes, found incredibly rich gold and silver deposits in an old prospect hole in 1877. A town called Bassickville grew up around the mine, which yielded a half million dollars in ore in two years. The town's name was changed to Querida ("darling" in Spanish) after Bassick sold his mine in 1879. Querida went into decline when legal battles closed the Bassick. When it reopened around the turn of the century, the town's glory days had passed, although the mine was worked into the 1920s.

Rosita

Rosita is southwest of Querida. Continue on Road 341 for 3.2 miles to Road 328, Rosita Road. At 4.6 miles from Querida, you will see the first mine diggings on your right, and .3 of a mile later you will arrive at the modest townsite of Rosita.

Rosita was founded in 1873 and named by miners for the thickets of wild roses that grew around the site's natural springs. By the middle of the decade it had about fifteen hundred people. From 1878 until 1886 it was the seat of Custer County, named for the general who had died at Little Big Horn in 1876.

Several modern cabins and homes, along with some cabin ruins, make up Rosita today. A nicely restored cabin, marked "Assay Office," stands near the road.

The Rosita Cemetery is almost a mile west of town. One poignant grave marker is a double stone with two lambs for John and James Baker, born a year apart, who died on the same day in 1882. Neither saw his third birthday.

When You Go

Westcliffe is 57 miles southeast of Salida. Take U.S. 50 east for 31 miles to Texas Creek and head south on State Route 69. A lovely shortcut through Cotopaxi cuts off 11 miles (consult a map). See text for further directions to the towns in this section.

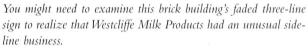
You might need to examine this brick building's faded three-line sign to realize that Westcliffe Milk Products had an unusual side-line business.

A magnificent old stove still resides inside a deserted home in Silver Cliff.

This 1883 photograph of Silver Cliff shows a well-dressed class of men, many likely posing proudly near their businesses. The two men in front of the jewelry store, for example, might be Mr. Chester and Mr. Cornwell themselves—note the watch fob conspicuously hanging from the pocket of the gentleman leaning on the post. Note also the proud owner of a high-wheeled Penny Farthing bicycle. (Courtesy of the Ted Kierscey Photo Collection.)

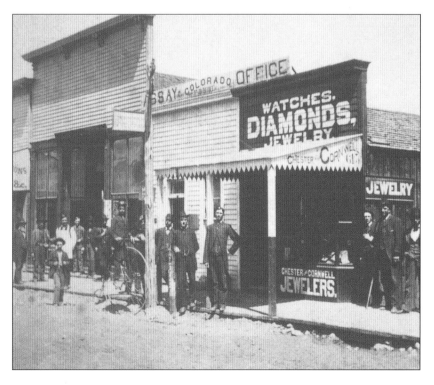

Chapter Eight

CRIPPLE CREEK GHOSTS

Left: *A common way to try to insulate older buildings in more modern times was to cover them with tarpaper. Fortunately for photographers, this relic in Goldfield has shed most of its wrapping.*

Above: *The most frequently visited grave in Cripple Creek's Mount Pisgah Cemetery belongs to madam Pearl DeVere. Her grave is often covered with candles, poems, coins, and flowers.*

Although the Gold Rush of 1859 was known for "Pikes Peak or Bust," the early discoveries were sixty miles northwest of that mountain. More than thirty years later, prospectors made a serious attempt to ascertain what lay in Pikes Peak's shadow. The reminders of the resulting bonanza are described in this chapter, including Cripple Creek, now a lively casino town; Victor, one of Colorado's largest and best-preserved mining camps; and several of their ghostly suburbs.

Cripple Creek

Cripple Creek practically saved Colorado. When the Silver State was reeling from the Silver Crash of 1893, Cripple Creek was alive and thriving because gold, not silver, surrounded the town.

The colorful name supposedly came from a mishap involving a cowboy on horseback chasing a cow into a creek, a chase that resulted in a broken leg to the horse and cow and a broken arm to the cowboy. On hearing the account, a wag is supposed to have remarked something like, "That is a Cripple Creek."

Prospectors began to explore the area in 1874, but little was found. This wasn't a place where gold should appear. The geology seemed wrong, and the deposits were hard to extract. The place confounded prospectors, confused miners, and made speculators poor. In 1884, a local scam brought investors to salted claims. As a result, the hills around Mount Pisgah had a tainted reputation.

The area became better known for its ranching and included ranch property owned by Horace Bennett and Julius Myers. When prospectors once again tried the Mount Pisgah District in 1891, Bennett and Myers platted a town near the claims, named the two main streets after themselves and the town itself after explorer John C. Fremont.

A rival community, Hayden Placer, grew near Fremont, but ultimately the two joined, choosing the name everyone was using already: Cripple Creek. A bonanza was forecast.

Bob Womack, the original owner of part of Bennett and Myers's ranch, is credited with finding the first promising ore, though he reportedly sold out his claims for a few hundred dollars before the true bonanzas were discovered. Another sometime Cripple

From a distance, Cripple Creek looks little different than it did before limited-stakes gambling came to town. The magnificent Sangre de Cristo Mountains form the backdrop.

Creek prospector, Colorado Springs carpenter Winfield Scott Stratton, persisted in his search for the major lode. He found it southeast of Cripple Creek on Battle Mountain when he made the Independence claim on July 4, 1891. He became a multimillionaire even as Silver King Horace Tabor was losing everything in Leadville.

Cripple Creek boomed as silver towns floundered. Fortunately for laid-off silver miners, they could be gold miners as well, and they were Cripple Creek bound.

By 1894, the town was approaching city status with electricity, telegraph service, telephones, and a population of six thousand. The mines had produced $5 million in gold as improved technology assisted in processing ore. Another boost came that year with the arrival of David Moffat's Florence & Cripple Creek Railroad, followed a

Oil lamps lit a miner's way through the dark tunnels. This one features a "bull's eye" lens.

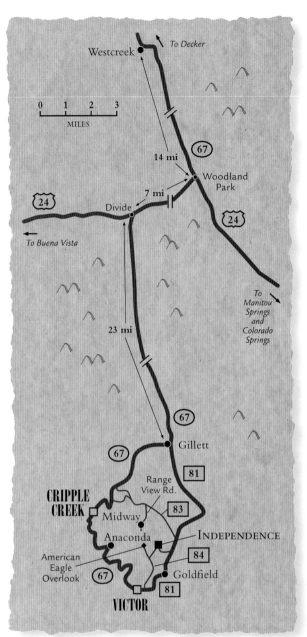

year later by the Midland Terminal Railroad. Not only could ore be more efficiently processed, but it also could be more cheaply shipped.

Two disastrous fires only four days apart in April 1896 destroyed fifteen acres of downtown and residential Cripple Creek. Rebuilding began immediately—with brick. A year later Cripple Creek's mayor declared the fire a "blessing in disguise," since the community was no longer a clapboard mining town but rather a modern city. Cripple Creek became a Colorado jewel.

In that same year, the district produced an amazing $7.4 million in gold; it hit its peak in 1900 at $18 million, when Cripple Creek was Colorado's fourth-largest city.

Cripple Creek became the second-largest gold district in U.S. history, with about twenty-one million ounces of gold extricated, worth over $8 billion in 1998 dollars. And it is not finished, at least at this writing. An open pit operation that began in 1995 is chewing into many legendary mines, which will add to the gold-production total. Unfortunately, it is also chewing into some old mining camps.

Walking and Driving Around Cripple Creek

Like Central City and Black Hawk, Cripple Creek is now a casino town, and street parking is nearly nonexistent. A good place to begin your stay is to visit the Cripple Creek District Museum. Not only is it an excellent museum, it allows you a short-term place to park.

The museum is located in the former Midland Terminal Depot, which was constructed in 1896. In the peak years, ten passenger trains, including ones from Denver featuring sleeping cars and a champagne dinner, came to this depot every day. Almost sixty trains per day went from Cripple Creek to Victor. Rail service ended in 1949, and four years later the nonprofit, private museum was established in the depot.

The museum has displays of mining equipment,

107

historic photos, and paraphernalia such as an old telephone switchboard. While there, ask for a handout for the Mount Pisgah Cemetery. In that cemetery is the replacement headstone for Pearl DeVere. The original wooden marker is housed in the museum. Ask for directions to see that marker.

Pearl DeVere was a madam of the Old Homestead, which served Cripple Creek's well-to-do males as the town's most exclusive brothel. Pearl died of a morphine overdose in 1897, apparently after she had been forsaken by her lover. Her funeral was a remarkable affair, with the Elks Band marching in her cortege to the cemetery playing "Good-bye, Little Girl, Good-bye." It was the longest such procession in Cripple Creek's history.

The museum's third floor is filled with Victorian furniture; when you visit it, look from the balcony for an outstanding view down Bennett Avenue. Also on that floor is the Governor Carr Room. Cripple Creek resident Ralph Carr was governor of Colorado from 1939 until 1943. He took a courageous but then-unpopular

stance regarding Japanese Americans during World War II, saying, "They are loyal Americans, sharing only race with the enemy."

The Colorado Trading and Transfer Building, the only wooden structure on Bennett Avenue spared in the 1896 fires, is next door to the museum. It currently houses the Heritage Gallery and the museum's gift shop, where you can purchase an extremely useful (and inexpensive) paperback book, *Cripple Creek: City of Influence*. This book has dozens of historic and current photographs and features a business district walking tour and two residential driving tours.

Walking down Bennett Avenue gives you a good feel for Cripple Creek's past, because many buildings have historical plaques. While you walk, notice the elaborate cornices and towers atop many edifices.

In the town's heyday, the businesses were varied, as they were when I first saw the town in the 1970s. But crafts shops, ice cream parlors, and antique stores have been universally replaced by casinos. As you read the

Both Cripple Creek and Victor have elaborate signs painted on brick walls. This one is in Cripple Creek. Note also the elegant tower on the Weinberg Block and the ornate cornices on both the Weinberg and Aspen Blocks. When rebuilding took place in 1896 after a disastrous fire, owners of the new structures outdid each other with showpiece Victorian touches.

plaques, you will be serenaded, if that's the right word, by the constant electronic whirring and bonging of countless gaming machines.

A block south of Bennett on Myers Avenue, once the notorious red light district, is the Old Homestead, Pearl DeVere's "house." Now a museum, the 1896 structure is open for reasonably priced tours. The brothel contains hundreds of original items, from dresses to furniture to ornate fixtures. I found the place fascinating, with its special screens and rooms to conceal dignitaries. The tour, incidentally, was done with decorum; considering the subject matter, I'd give it a "G" rating. I did, however, think what questions my ever-curious daughter might have asked years ago if she had taken the tour as a child ("Daddy, what exactly would these women do for the men who visited?"). Use your judgment with younger children.

North of Bennett are many interesting buildings, such as the homes clustered around Fourth and Carr. Northwest of these homes are the 1897 St. Nicholas Hospital (now a hotel) and the 1892 St. Peter's Catholic Church, both near Eaton and Third.

At 127 West Carr, a few blocks southwest of the church, is the lovely 1897 Miller House, Cripple Creek's most elegant residence. From there, go west to "B" Street and continue north to its end to see the former Teller County Hospital, built in 1901, with its unusual external stairway to the second story.

After exploring the town, take the short drive to Mount Pisgah Cemetery, on the main road heading west from town. With views of nearby Mount Pisgah and Cripple Creek, this is one of the prettiest cemeteries in Colorado. It is also one of the best maintained, thanks to the efforts of volunteers.

As in other pioneer graveyards, a large number of stones are for children. A particularly moving one was for the sons of Mr. and Mrs. Ellis: "When God came for Baby Rexford, We prayed that was All. But There came another Message and to Him our Ralphie called." Rexford died in 1895 at ten months; four-year-old Ralphie died the next year.

To find Pearl DeVere's grave, take the main drive through the south side of the cemetery, proceeding west until you see a series of soldiers' graves on your right. Keep going until you find a headstone on your left with

The doll and buggy (left) belonged to Cripple Creek native Myla Orr, who died in 1997 at age eighty-one. Her sister Gladys owned the large German-made doll on the right. The dolls reside on the third floor of the Cripple Creek District Museum, where there is a display depicting a Victorian home.

an open Bible carved on top. Park and walk a few yards southwest to a wrought iron fence. Pearl's grave is next to it.

When You Go

To reach Cripple Creek from Colorado Springs, take State Route 24 west for 25 miles to the town of Divide. Go south 28 miles on State Route 67.

Anaconda

The Anaconda Mine was discovered in 1894. Its namesake was a successful Montana mine, which in turn was named for Union General Winfield Scott's strategy during the Civil War of encircling the enemy like the South American snake.

The town of Anaconda also housed miners of the Jack Pot, Doctor, and Mary McKinney Mines. Its most famous citizen was Mary Louise Guinan, an aspiring actress who went to New York City and instead became Texas Guinan, Queen of the Speakeasies. Her saloon greeting, "Hello, Sucker!" became popular slang of the Roaring Twenties.

Anaconda was largely destroyed by fire in 1904 and never rebuilt. A few structures stand today, protected by a

Cripple Creek Attractions

Here are three additional Cripple Creek attractions worth considering.

Mollie Kathleen Mine Tour

This is second only to the Old Hundred Mine near Silverton (see chapter ten) as the best mine tour I took in Colorado. You descend a thousand feet in a double cage into the mine itself. The guides are former miners, and ours was particularly good with an adventurous child, keeping him fascinated without letting him be disruptive. I considered the hour-long tour a good value compared to other similar tours. The mine is located north of town along the highway.

Cripple Creek & Victor Narrow Gauge Railroad

This steam-driven train begins next door to the museum. The route goes two miles south to the sparse remains of Anaconda. This ride is actually the best way to see Anaconda because of the railroad's vantage point. The ride is short but inexpensive.

This enormous ore-sorting house separated ore from waste prior to milling at the Mollie Kathleen Mine. Despite its antique look, the building was constructed in the 1940s or 1950s.

The Gold Belt Tour

This marvelous back-roads drive is free. Basically, it takes the Shelf Road south from Cripple Creek, goes to Cañon City, and returns via Phantom Canyon Road. Phantom Canyon Road is passable in normal weather for a passenger car. I'd recommend a high-clearance vehicle for the Shelf Road.

To reach the Shelf Road, drive south from downtown Cripple Creek on State Route 67 toward Victor. In only .2 of a mile from Bennett and Second, take Teller County Road 88, the dirt road heading to the right. The stream you will be driving parallel to is the actual Cripple Creek. Phantom Canyon Road (Teller County Road 86) comes out on the southeast end of Victor.

Cripple Creek & Victor Narrow Gauge Railroad Engine #1 awaits passengers in Cripple Creek. The locomotive was built in Germany in 1902 and was formerly used in a Mexican mining operation. The train departs from a station built in Anaconda in 1894; it moved to its present site in 1968.

fence and "No Trespassing" signs. Although you can see them from the road, you can get a better view from the Cripple Creek & Victor Narrow Gauge Railroad ride out of Cripple Creek.

A blacksmith shop with a cupola roof stands above the highway. Across a draw is a building with a rock wall attached that was the powder magazine, and the company office stands above it. Below the road, near some trees, are the rock foundations of the jail.

When You Go

Anaconda is 2 miles southeast of Cripple Creek on Road 67 to Victor. It sits above the highway as you make a horseshoe turn.

Victor

Victor was founded in 1893 and named by Harry Woods for the nearby Victor Mine. Another account says it was named for homesteader Victor Adams.

Cripple Creek was home to investors and mine owners, while Victor was a miners' town. As a result, Victor became Cripple Creek's natural rival, and therefore enjoyed any chance for one-upmanship. For instance, in 1897, Victor entered a float in a Salt Lake City festival with the Queen of Victor aboard. She generously invited the Cripple Creek Queen to ride as well. The *Victor Daily Record* wryly noted, "We might say that Cripple Creek took a ride on Victor's band wagon, but Cripple has often done that commercially and the habit is growing."

Victor surpassed its rival in size for a short time, but it took the Cripple Creek fires of 1896 to do it. When Cripple Creek rebuilt, it was again larger and even grander. When a fire decimated Victor in 1899, it also rebuilt, but its best times were already over.

Victor, however, was something special in its prime. The Portland Mine was "Queen of the District," producing half of Battle Mountain's gold. One of its muckers was a kid named William Dempsey, who would become famous as a boxer under his brother's name, Jack.

Ore was found all around Victor and even within the city itself. The workings were so rich that supposedly worthless tailings were used to pave Victor's streets. When Harry Woods and his brother Frank were excavating a foundation for the Victor Hotel, they discovered a rich ore body. The hotel plan was shelved, and the Gold Coin Mine opened, eventually yielding $6 million in gold. After the Gold Coin's buildings were destroyed in the 1899 fire, the Woods brothers rebuilt the shaft house with ornate touches such as stained glass windows. Their showy gesture demonstrated their confidence in the district. That

confidence was ill founded, however; within a few years, the brothers were bankrupt.

Deteriorating ore bodies and labor troubles initiated Victor's decline. As a miners' town, it became the center for labor unrest when the Western Federation of Miners attempted to standardize wages and shorten the working day. Strikes and violence slowed production of nearly pinched-out mines. When miners left practically en masse to join World War I, Battle Mountain mines never recovered. The only other "mining" Victor did was during the Depression, when the low-grade ore that had been used to pave the streets was scraped up and milled.

Walking and Driving Around Victor

Although Cripple Creek has succumbed to the glitter of casino gambling, Victor remains authentic—a bit dowdy, even dilapidated, but completely delightful. For me, that makes Victor one of the West's best mining towns.

Attractions for the ghost town enthusiast abound, including the Lowell Thomas Museum, on the southeast corner of Third and Victor Avenue, the main road through town. There you will find interesting memorabilia and items about Lowell Thomas, a Victor High School graduate whose radio voice became familiar to millions of Americans. That same intersection features the Fortune Club on the southwest corner, with an elaborate painted advertisement on its wall. South on Third from the Fortune Club is the Isis Theater, a turn-of-the-century building that went from live theater to silent movies to talkies. Its sloping floor still has several rows of theater seats.

Farther down Victor Avenue at Fourth stands the Victor Hotel, originally a bank. It has a huge vault in the lobby and a wonderful elevator.

South of the Victor Hotel on Fourth are several outstanding buildings, including the Masonic Hall, with its three elaborate Colonial Revival cornices; the office of the *Victor Record*; and the Christian Science church, originally a saloon and bowling alley.

Drive the back streets south of the main business district to see countless boomtown-era homes that range from the abandoned to the neglected to the carefully restored.

North of Victor Avenue on Fourth, as you head toward the foothills of Battle Mountain, you will see Pikes Peak Power Company Substation #1 on your left, and, at Fourth and Diamond, the once-elegant Gold Coin Club. Built for the workers of the Gold Coin Mine, the club featured a library, bowling alley, and swimming pool. The mine itself, the one discovered by the Woods brothers while building the foundation for a hotel, is across the street.

The headframe of the Independence Mine stands on Battle Mountain above Victor. Several buildings are easily identifiable, including the city hall (left, middle, with the gold dome). Directly behind it is Pikes Peak Power Company Substation #1. The tallest building, with the arching, third-story windows, is the Victor Hotel, originally a bank.

The sign for the Elks section of Victor's Sunnyside Cemetery frames the Sangre de Cristo Mountains. Four fraternal groups have their own sections: Moose, Odd Fellows, Eagles, and Elks.

South of Victor Avenue on Fourth Street stand several historic buildings. The one with the triple cornices (center) is the Masonic Hall. Across the street and down the block is the still-active First Baptist Church (far right).

Continue east on Diamond and then north one block to see the Midland Terminal Railway Depot, which is now a private residence.

As you head west toward Cripple Creek, you will see another fine building on Victor Avenue—the 1900 city hall with its ornate tower. West of the city hall .1 of a mile is the turnoff south to the cemetery, less than a mile away.

Victor's Sunnyside Cemetery features a rather large number of wooden markers surrounded by wrought iron fences.

When You Go

Victor is 6 miles southeast of Cripple Creek on State Route 67 and 7.4 miles south of Gillett on Road 81.

Incidentally, there once was another way to get from Cripple Creek to Victor. Battle Mountain is so extensively tunneled that one could actually walk between the two cities completely underground.

Independence and Midway

A short tour from Victor offers two sites that were satellite communities on Battle Mountain. Much of the property you will be traversing is owned by the Cripple Creek and Victor Gold Mining Company, and future operations could change the landscape considerably. Independence and Midway could disappear, joining extinct towns such as Elkton, Beacon Hill, Altman, Stratton, and Cameron.

County Road 84 heads north from Victor past chutes, foundations of oil tanks, and the Independence headframe. In 1.5 miles you will come to the turnoff to the town of Independence. You won't take this road now, but you will turn here on the way back down.

Continue up the main road for another mile to the American Eagle Overlook. From here you have a view that includes the current mine, the Sangre de Cristo

At this writing, more than four dozen dilapidated structures stand, or lean, at Independence. Most are small, wood-frame cabins, but this residence was the home of the mine superintendent. Barely visible behind the roof is the headframe of the Vindicator Mine. In the background is the enormous Vindicator sorting house. Although the house was no doubt comfortable, this would have been a very noisy place to live.

Mountains, the west end of Cripple Creek, and, to the east, the upper part of Goldfield.

The American Eagle Mine was purchased by gold magnate Winfield S. Stratton in 1895. At the mine site today are several buildings, including a residence, blacksmith shop, and the shifter's office (where the "shifter" made certain that lessee and owner each received his share of a shift's ore). Also on the site is a headframe, along with pulleys, winches, and cables.

Return to the turnoff to Independence and proceed to the site.

Independence

Independence was founded in 1894 and named for the nearby Independence Mine, Winfield S. Stratton's greatest producer.

The town's most infamous moment occurred June 6, 1904, when professional terrorist Harry Orchard, employed by the Western Federation of Miners, blew up the railroad station at Independence. The explosion was timed for a maximum number of strikebreaking miners to be waiting for a train. Thirteen were killed and many more grievously injured.

As a result, mine company thugs wrecked the office of the *Victor Record*, which was considered sympathetic to the union, and rounded up seventy-three strikers who were taken to the Kansas border and abandoned. The union was defeated when nonunion labor replaced the strikers. Orchard's act backfired. He also killed one of his own: Alexander McLean, a Western Federation member, died in the blast and was buried with honors by the union and the Woodmen of the World in the Mount Pisgah Cemetery.

From Independence, continue until you reach Road 81, which connects Gillett and Victor. A large, two-story brick residence will be on your left.

(Note: If you are leaving this area and not returning, visit Goldfield, the next entry, before you continue on this loop. Goldfield is less than a mile south on Road 81.)

At the junction of the Independence road and Road 81, note your mileage and turn left onto Road 83 heading northwest. In 2.3 miles, turn left onto Range View Road. A sign will indicate that the road is closed ahead, but continue anyway. In a half mile you will pass the mining company field offices.

Midway

Beyond those offices .3 of a mile is the tiny site of Midway, which contains two cabins with a small tin shack nearby, a stone structure on a hill, and the Grand View Saloon, a deteriorating false-front store once popular as an end-of-shift stop for miners. The place was "midway" between Cripple Creek and Victor.

Back at Road 83, you can turn right to return to Victor or left to reach Cripple Creek, 3.4 miles away. To go to Cripple Creek, take Road 83 until it comes to a fork. Take the left fork and follow it to Highway 67.

When You Go

From Victor, head toward Goldfield and turn left onto Road 84. Then follow directions in the text.

Goldfield

Goldfield was a carefully platted company town, erected in 1894 for workers in the Portland Mine, Battle Mountain's greatest producer. As a workers' town, it was torn by the same union-management confrontations that went to the very bone of Independence and Victor. Looking at Goldfield today, one wonders how it could have had five hotels, four churches, five grocery stores, three schools, and a population of three thousand.

Only one notable building remains, the 1899 city hall and fire station, three blocks east of the main road. Its fire bell and hose drying tower stands in the back right corner, not the usual front and center. About twenty empty buildings, along with another dozen or so occupied, apparently date from the town's heyday.

When You Go

Goldfield is 1.1 miles northeast of Victor on Road 81.

Gillett

Gillett was created in 1894 as a stop along the Midland Terminal Railroad. Named for W. K. Gillett, eventual president of the line, the town had smelters and reduction mills for Cripple Creek District mines.

Gillett was not merely a smelter city, however. It was a sporting center, with its Monte Carlo Casino, racetrack, fourteen saloons, and the West's only bull ring. The latter was reportedly used only once, as the spectacle horrified onlookers. Originally known as a bachelors' town, the place eventually settled down—the casino became the Gillett School.

Three buildings of apparent antiquity make up Gillett—a two-story house, a one-story, and an outbuilding behind the two. Stone ruins stand on a northern hill. Much of the land was for sale in 1997, so what Gillett will look like in the future is anyone's guess.

When You Go

Gillett stands where State Route 67 heads 5 miles southwest to Cripple Creek and Road 81 goes 7.4 miles south to Victor.

Westcreek

When gold was found along West Creek in 1895, two townsites were created: Pemberton and Tyler, each named for the ranch it stood on. Six other camps formed as well, as prospectors hunted for an extension of the fabulous Cripple Creek ore body. The name of one camp spoke the hopes of all—North Cripple Creek. Only Pemberton had a post office, opened the following January. In 1902, its name was changed to West Creek, later shortened to Westcreek.

The West Creek district had as many as five thousand prospectors, and every new find would cause them to dash from camp to camp. The only people who seemed to find prosperity were two women selling freshly baked bread for fifteen cents a loaf.

As you leave the highway to enter Westcreek, you will see two log cabins up a driveway to your left. Proceed to the stop sign at West Creek Road. To the left are modern cabins, homes, a man-made lake, and a fire station. To the right, up the road about .3 of a mile, are seven original wood-frame buildings in various states of decay. (These buildings are posted against trespassing.)

The Westcreek Cemetery contains about three dozen graves, many of which are marked by only a simple metal rod. A particularly poignant headstone is for Sondra Kay Stodghill, born December 7, 1943. The stone is engraved with baby booties and a teddy bear, as Sondra Kay lived only until March 14, 1944.

When You Go

Westcreek is 14 miles northwest of Woodland Park on State Route 67. Turn west on the side road. The cemetery is north of the highway .9 of a mile before that turnoff.

Chapter Nine

LAKE CITY GHOSTS

Left: *Several dozen buildings, most of them miners' cabins, stand at Summitville today. The initial boom only lasted from 1870 until 1889, but gold was still being extracted from its mines into the 1970s.*

Above: *A marker on the east side of Lake City commemorates the five men murdered and cannibalized by Alferd Packer.*

The mining towns of Hinsdale County vary from appealing Lake City to pure ghost Carson to "place-where" sites Sherman and Capitol City. Add Mineral County's Creede and its scenic Bachelor Historic Loop, along with Rio Grande County's Summitville, and here is a chapter ideal for ghost-town exploring.

Lake City

Lake City rivals Georgetown as one of Colorado's most charming communities. Although smaller than Georgetown and not quite as splendid, it is also not nearly as crowded or tourist oriented. Its downtown has some delightful buildings, while residential areas feature attractive homes and churches.

The region's most infamous incident occurred in late 1873 or early 1874, before Lake City existed. Alferd Packer was hired by Utah prospectors to guide them through the San Juan Mountains. Many gave up as winter approached, but five continued with Packer. Two months later, when he arrived, alone, at Los Pinos Indian Agency, Packer claimed he had become separated from his companions and had nearly starved.

A search party found the men near Lake San Cristobal. All were dead, four from ax blows, the fifth from a bullet. All had been, literally, butchered. Remembering that the "nearly starved" Packer had seemed suspiciously well fed, the would-be rescuers reached a logical but grisly conclusion. Packer, however, had vanished.

Meanwhile, other prospectors were also combing the San Juans. The area's mineral deposits were spotted in 1874 by surveyor Enos Hotchkiss while scouting a wagon route through the San Juans. He and his party abandoned the road project and spent the winter staking claims.

By the spring of 1875, a camp of four hundred citizens was firmly established where Hotchkiss's party had settled. Hotchkiss returned to road building long enough to create a toll road from Saguache with partner Otto Mears, the "Pathfinder of the San Juans" (see chapter ten).

Improved roads meant cheaper transportation of ore, and the camp, called Lake City for Lake San Cristobal, boomed. Also in 1875, the town wrested the seat of recently created Hinsdale County from San Juan City, which has since disappeared.

The arrival of the Denver & Rio Grande Railroad in the late 1880s added to Lake City's status.

Carbide Justrite Victor Cap Lamps assisted miners in their labors.

One hopes these gentlemen were trying to be humorous, not dignified, with their serious pose on Lake City's Silver Street. After all, their noble steed is a donkey, and instead of using a proper harness, they merely attached a rope to the saddle. But as they sleigh, or rather sled, through town, at least their donkey will have the traditional sleighbell sound. Are the men along the boardwalk watching in admiration, or are they guffawing? (Courtesy of the Ted Kierscey Photo Collection.)

The town boasted five general stores, five saloons, three restaurants, three breweries, two drugstores, two bakeries, two blacksmith shops, two meat markets, a newspaper, and a public library.

Back to unfinished business. In 1883, nine years after he had been suspected of murder and cannibalism, Alferd Packer was apprehended in Wyoming and brought to Lake City for trial. When Packer left camp near Lake San Cristobal, there was no Lake City; less than a decade later, he was being tried in its two-story courthouse. He was found guilty of murder and sentenced to death, but the sentence was later reduced to a prison term. After serving several years, Packer was paroled.

The Silver Crash of 1893 damaged Lake City, but enough gold was also being mined that the town held on into the new century.

Walking and Driving Around Lake City

At the south end of Lake City's business district, at Silver and Second Streets, is the Hinsdale County Museum. It is housed in the Finley Block, a single stone building constructed by stonemason Henry Finley, who fashioned the attractive storefront himself.

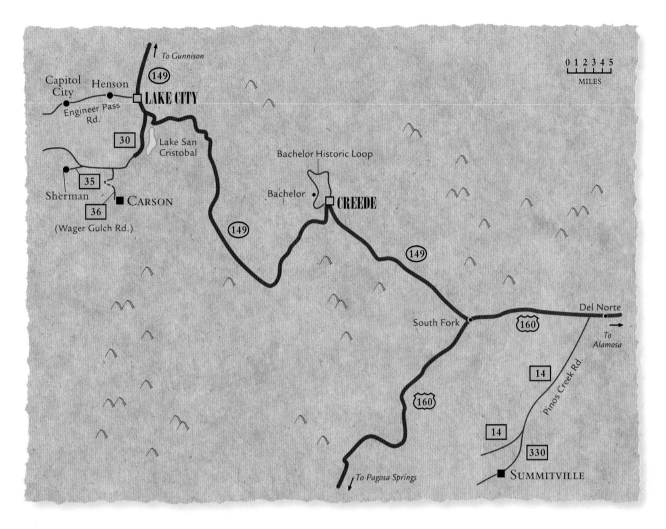

The museum has many unusual items and displays. For example, one display profiles Susan B. Anthony's visit to Lake City in 1877; another shows a doll house made by Alferd Packer while he was in prison. One exhibit showcases the Hough Firefighters, which were sponsored by John Simpson Hough, a prosperous entrepreneur. His backing of the fire department was a public-spirited thing to do—and practical, because the firefighters protected his investments as well those of others.

Downtown Lake City features several other historic buildings. At the corner of Silver and Third stands the 1877 Stone Bank Block, which served as a bank until 1914. It was then converted to other uses, including a forty-year stint as a hotel. Around the corner is Armory Hall, originally the 1883 opera house. The restricted, posh Hinsdale Club for men used the building's second floor.

The Hough Block, on the east side of Silver in the next block north, was built by John Hough between 1880 and 1882. For Lake City old-timers, however, the block is remembered for Mike and Stella Pavich, who purchased the building in 1932 and ran Mike's Place Cafe there until 1945, when they turned it into a grocery.

The 1877 Hinsdale County Courthouse is one block east of the highway, between Third and Fourth Streets. The first floor corridor displays documents on the Alferd Packer trial. The second-floor courtroom, except for a microphone and computer, transports you to 1877.

Too many historic residences stand in Lake City to enumerate them all, but here are several of my favorites. At the northeast corner of Fifth and Gunnison (State Route 149) is the 1877 John Hough House. Across the street is the small 1876 Episcopal Chapel, originally a carpentry shop. South of the chapel is the lovely 1877 Turner House at 513 Gunnison. (Turner and a partner operated the carpentry shop that later became the chapel.)

The most grandiose residence in town, the 1892 Youmans House, stands on the northeast corner of Sixth and Gunnison. A plaque in front of the elaborately ornate, two-story home wryly states that the home was "intended to be noticed."

Henry Kohler's brick home stands on the northeast corner of Fifth and Silver. Kohler, a pharmacist, returned to his native Germany for his bride and built this home for her as a wedding present.

Three attractive churches remain in Lake City. The Presbyterian church, built in 1876, is located on Fifth

Above: *The Lake City Cemetery has several interesting graves and many ornamental iron fences. One grave in the southeast corner (not shown) has a board marker with the faded inscription "Our Baby—in Memory of Alfred Pedersen. Born June the 30th 1882. Died August the 13th 1882. Blessed Be Thy Sleep." An enormous pine tree grows inside the small enclosure.*

Left: *Lake City's Silver Street has excellent examples of clapboard commercial buildings. Each features an attractive cornice atop its false front.*

near Gunnison. The narthex and steeple were added in 1882, with side doors flanking a decorative center window. It was aesthetic, perhaps, but not practical—caskets could not fit through the side doors. The window was replaced with a main door that gave pallbearers a straight shot into the church.

The 1891 First Baptist Church, on Bluff Street at Fourth, can accommodate almost two hundred worshipers.

The third church, one few visitors see, is the St. Rose of Lima Catholic Church. To reach it, cross Henson Creek bridge on the south side of town and turn west through the Henson Creek RV Park. The church was built in 1878 and restored between 1982 and 1992. Beyond it stands a handsome mansard-roofed brick home.

South of town 2.8 miles on State Route 149 is the Alferd Packer Massacre Site. Five metal crosses mark where Israel Swan, George Swan, Frank Miller, James Humphreys, and Wilson Bell were murdered.

The Lake City Cemetery is located a mile north of downtown along the highway. Another cemetery is a half mile away. From the Lake City Cemetery, head north

First Baptist Church's forty-five-foot-high steeple and lovely stained-glass windows make it one of Lake City's most attractive places of worship.

and then immediately turn left onto Balsam Drive, following the road to a wooden fence.

The Hinsdale–I. O. O. F. Cemetery has hundreds of graves. Two markers recall mining's dangers. Harry Pierce died in an explosion at the Ulay Mine in 1878. Judson Hillis died in 1890 "as a result of an accident in the Ulay Mill on Henson Creek."

A grave on a hill in the northwest corner affected me enormously. It is for Roger David Coursey, age forty-four, who "gave his life in the line of duty November 18, 1994." I was so touched by the stone and its inscriptions that I returned to the sheriff's office (located in a building dedicated to Coursey) to learn more.

Roger Coursey died ten days into his first elective term as Hinsdale County Sheriff after two men attempted to rob a bank in Creede. He and another officer stopped the men's car near the turnoff to the Packer Massacre Site. Sheriff Coursey was shot dead, leaving a wife and four children.

When You Go

Lake City is 54 miles southwest of Gunnison and 52 miles northwest of Creede on State Route 149.

Henson and Capitol City

Henson

Henson was named for prospector Henry Henson, who, along with three others, filed a claim in 1871 for the Ute-Ulay Mine. However, they could not exploit the claim until the Brunot Treaty of 1873 opened the San Juans to settlement.

Henson's group sold the mine in 1876 to Lake City's Crooke brothers for $125,000. They in turn sold in 1880 for $1.2 million, a tidy return on their investment. A town was platted near the mine and named for its discoverer. By that time Henry Henson was a senator, and he later became a judge.

Henson today is a ghost town on private property, but you can still see most of it, because the road to it bisects the town. As you enter Henson, south of the road you will see waste dumps, sheds, tanks, assorted mining equipment, a mill, and a mine building with two brick chimneys. Across the road are two log cabins, a two-story building that likely was a dormitory, and other sheds and cabins. On the west end of the site are more mine structures and a dam, now breached, extending across Henson Creek.

Capitol City

Capitol City, as the name implies, was meant for bigger things than the two frame buildings standing near the North Fork of Henson Creek would indicate. Originally it was called Galena City, but sawmill and smelter owner George S. Lee was so convinced that his fledgling town would supersede Denver that in 1877 he renamed it Capitol City (although he should have spelled it "capital"). He also built a two-story brick mansion, at the then-outrageous cost of a dollar a brick, in which he—as governor, naturally—and his wife would reside. (A photograph in Lake City's Hinsdale County Museum shows that the Lee Mansion, although in serious disrepair, survived into the 1950s.)

Although Capitol City never attained the glory Lee predicted, it did prosper until the 1893 Silver Crash. Gold was found in 1900, and a modest rebirth occurred.

When You Go

From Lake City, turn west on Second Street from Gunnison Avenue onto the road to Engineer Pass. Henson is 3.9 miles west. Capitol City is 5.4 miles beyond Henson. Although traveling the entire length of Engineer Pass demands a four-wheel-drive vehicle, the road between Lake City and Capitol City is suitable for passenger cars.

Carson

Like many other true ghost towns, Carson sits in an unspeakably beautiful setting. Like a few others, it is unoccupied. This combination makes Carson one of my favorite mining camps anywhere.

Christopher J. Carson, prospecting along the Conti-

A skeleton is all that remains of Carson's general store. Carson is the quintessential Colorado ghost town, with its striking, aged ruins and breathtaking scenery.

nental Divide, found gold and silver in 1881 and staked a claim for the Bonanza King. The small camp named for Carson struggled through the early 1880s because of transportation problems, but miners still managed to work 150 claims in which silver out-produced gold by a hundred ounces to one.

Transportation woes were eased when a road from Lake City was begun in 1883, led by an overseer named Wager, for whom the gulch was named. Another road from Wagon Wheel Gap reached the south side of the Divide in 1887.

The abundance of silver crippled Carson in 1893 when silver prices plummeted. But in 1896, promising gold deposits were found, bringing more than four hundred miners back, principally to the St. Jacobs and Bachelor Mines. At this time buildings were constructed north of the pass at a "new" Carson. "Old" Carson was on the south side. By 1902, however, the *Gunnison Times* reported, "Carson with its many promising properties is practically abandoned."

Standing at the new Carson today are seven structures, one made of logs and the others of cut lumber. The largest building was a boarding house for Bachelor Mine employees and may also have served as a hospital. It is interesting architecturally because it was built as if it were three separate structures connected by hallways. The walls were covered with graffiti, one reason why sites such as this become closed to the public.

Two nearby homes for the Bachelor Mine foreman and superintendent had tongue-in-groove interior woodwork, indicating that these buildings were not of slapdash construction. North of those homes is a buggy shed and stable.

The nearby Bachelor Mine is posted against trespassing, but you can see it nonetheless. Behind the Carson buildings is a faint trail that heads to the southeast. In perhaps thirty yards, you will come out behind the mine, where, without trespassing, you can view the operation, including a boiler, cable winch, dumps, and rotting boards.

Very little remains at old Carson, south of the Divide.

When this photo was taken of Carson in 1997, each of its seven standing buildings sported a recent metal roof, thanks to the owner. (Carson is on private property, but it was not posted against trespassing at that time.)

When Muriel Sibell Wolle hiked there in 1948, she saw mine buildings, houses, an old hotel, and the post office.

I learned one local legend about Carson from two young women doing lepidoptera studies nearby. They were told that when an influenza epidemic broke out in Carson, three women left the community during the winter to try to avoid the disease. They finally found a vacant cabin in a valley below where they tried to survive the winter. None caught influenza, but two died of starvation and the cold.

When you return from Carson, turn left on Road 30. The cabin where the three Carson women were supposed to have wintered is 3.3 miles west (on private property but visible along the north side of the road).

When You Go
From Lake City, head southeast on State Route 149 for 2.3 miles to Road 30, the turnoff to Lake San Cristobal and Cinnamon Pass. Drive 9 miles to Wager Gulch Road (Road 36), which goes south. The next 3.6 miles to Carson require a four-wheel-drive vehicle, especially in wet conditions.

Sherman

Sherman was platted in 1877 as a camp serving nearby gold and silver mines, including the Minnie Lee, Smile of Fortune, and the Black Wonder. The latter became the only solid producer, and Sherman prospered or failed largely based upon the fortunes of the Black Wonder, which operated into 1897.

Sherman, named for an early pioneer, featured streets sixty feet wide. Even alleys were twenty feet wide. But because the town was located at the confluence of the Lake Fork of the Gunnison River and Cottonwood Creek, Sherman repeatedly flooded. In about 1900, a dam was built upstream to control runoff, but it ruptured during the first cloudburst. Sherman was inundated and was never rebuilt.

The scant remnants of Sherman consist of scattered cabin ruins and the three-tiered rock wall foundation of the Black Wonder Mill, north of the road adjacent to a bridge crossing the Lake Fork of the Gunnison.

When You Go
Sherman is 4.2 miles west of Wager Gulch Road (the road to Carson). Take Road 30 for 3.5 miles and turn left onto Road 35. The Sherman townsite is .7 of a mile beyond that turn.

Creede

No one knew it then, but Creede would be "The Last of the Silver Towns." The area's bonanza began in 1890, a scant three years before the Silver Crash.

"Holy Moses!" Nicholas Creede is supposed have exclaimed to his partner when he found a rich silver outcropping in 1889. He staked his claim in that name. When David Moffat, Denver & Rio Grande Railroad president, toured the Holy Moses in 1890, he bought into the mine for sixty-five thousand dollars.

When others heard that a respected man such as Moffat was involved, the rush began. By the fall of 1890, houses, cabins, tents, and businesses lined Willow Creek for six miles with such density that one pioneer recalled there was not one square foot unstaked. Those lots were going at prices so outrageous that crafty settlers outsmarted lot owners by extending planks across Willow Creek and erecting shacks on them. Crafty it was, until the creek rose.

Several towns evolved along Willow Creek, including two of considerable size. The original Creede, up the canyon from the present town, became known as North Creede. South of that was Stringtown, followed by the other large settlement, Jimtown, which became present-day Creede. High above Jimtown to the west was Bachelor, the largest "suburb."

The effects of a century of mining and flooding show on the south end of Creede as Willow Creek (center, right) spills out into the Rio Grande. The red-roofed building (left, center) is an attractive modern high school built log-cabin style. The vacant church (middle, far right) is next to the Creede Cemetery. The canyon in sunlight (center, rear) is the beginning of the Rio Grande Palisades.

Bachelor Historic Tour

The Bachelor Historic Tour, named for the "suburb" high above and west of Creede, is one of the best scenic drives in the West. The loop requires a vehicle with reasonable power for a couple of steep grades, but in good weather a passenger car or van will certainly suffice.

The seventeen-mile tour begins at a kiosk "entrance station" south of Creede on State Route 149, where you can borrow or purchase an extremely well-written, well-illustrated booklet that will immeasurably enhance the route. Because you will have that booklet, I won't recount the highlights of the tour, except to say that you will gasp at the Commodore Mine buildings, early in the loop. Another stop will be at Bachelor, named for its single, male inhabitants. Today the site shows hardly a trace of its former vitality.

The next-to-last stop on your tour loop will be at the Creede Cemetery, which contains more wooden fences and markers than most Colorado graveyards.

The final stop of the tour is north of the cemetery, where Bob Ford, who gained ignominy for shooting Jesse James in the back, was buried, himself the recipient of a gunshot. His wife, however, had the body exhumed and taken to Missouri for reburial.

The first major stop along the Bachelor Historic Tour gives you a look at the Commodore Mine operation, one of the most dramatic ghost-town views in the West.

The Denver & Rio Grande arrived in 1891. Each new train brought as many as three hundred people to an already overcrowded Creede. Life moved at a frantic pace. A load of lumber one day was a store the next. Just five days after a groundbreaking for a power plant, Creede had electricity. As newspaper editor Cy Warman wrote in an oft-quoted poem, "It is day all day in the day-time / And there is no night in Creede."

Floods and fires plagued Creede and Jimtown because of their locations in or near narrow, deep canyons. Mere cloudbursts would send torrents of water through both towns. A saloon fire in 1892 reduced most of Jimtown's business district to charred sticks.

In 1893, Jimtown, by then called Creede, had a reported ten thousand citizens. They took the seat of newly created Mineral County from now-vanished Wason. Legend says they seized more than the seat—piece by piece, they moved the courthouse as well.

The demonetization of silver in 1893 ended Creede's bonanza, and by 1900 fewer than a thousand residents remained in Creede. Although the boom was over, significant mining continued off and on until 1985. The current population is less than four hundred.

And what became of Nicholas Creede, who began the bonanza? In 1897, he committed suicide with a morphine overdose in Los Angeles because, a contemporary report stated, "his wife, from whom he had separated, insisted on living with him."

Walking and Driving Around Creede

Creede's 1891 railroad depot, in the middle of town on Main Street, now houses a museum that features old photographs, a hand-drawn fire truck, a hearse, gaming tables, and other interesting items, including a piano that came to Creede by wagon. The piano was last played by Chester Brubacher, who didn't read music. To fill the music stand in front of his eyes, Chester placed a Sears catalog on it.

When he played happy music, he turned the catalog to women's bras. When he played a sad song, he paged over to the corset section.

Downtown Creede has several other attractive buildings, including the Creede Hotel, the tin false-fronted Quiller Gallery, and a mercantile that was later the firehouse (now a bed and breakfast inn).

When You Go
Creede is 52 miles southeast of Lake City and 27 miles northwest of South Fork on State Route 149.

Summitville

Summitville still hums with activity. However, it is not mining causing all the action; it is the removal of mining's detritus. Summitville is one of Colorado's several environmental Superfund sites, and the clean-up operation is immense. The ghost town, however, is apparently not part of the site, and there remains much to see. Summitville is also a natural candidate for another kind of "superfund"—preservation money from Colorado's gaming dollars.

In 1870, rancher James Esmund and a companion rode his horse into a high, parklike area in search of two runaway girls. They found the girls, and Esmund found something else—free gold in the rocks all around. He returned several times to remove high-grade ore, but unfortunately he neglected to file claims.

In June 1870, a party of prospectors, including James and William Wightman, staked claims along the creek now named for the brothers. Winter drove them out, but the next spring brought hundreds of argonauts. In 1872, hundreds more arrived, so when James Esmund returned once again, he discovered people swarming over the area, including his find, by then known as the Little Annie. He nevertheless staked claims for the Esmund (later the Aztec) and the Major Mines.

Summitville received its post office in 1876. By 1883, it was Colorado's biggest gold producer, occupying several hundred miners and millworkers for hugely successful mines, such as the Little Annie and the Bonanza. By 1889, however, the boom was over and only a few diehards remained.

A short-lived rebirth came in the late 1890s with the reopening of the Bonanza, but the mine's production fizzled by 1900. Miners tried again to resurrect Summitville for two years beginning in 1911, for five years starting in 1926, and for about fifteen years commencing in the 1930s.

Another attempt was beginning after World War II, when Muriel Sibell Wolle visited Summitville. She was expecting a ghost town but found instead a company town of tarpaper-covered shacks and a large community hall flying an American flag.

Further attempts were made in the 1970s, but not even the discovery of a boulder containing $350,000 in gold lying near a road could revitalize the town.

When you arrive in Summitville today, you will see a cluster of about a dozen residences and outbuildings on a small hill south of the road. At this writing, the wood-frame structures are under roof and partially covered with tarpaper. One of the buildings enclosed a water pump, a necessity at 11,300 feet.

About .3 of a mile down the road is a second group of structures even more interesting than the first. On the left, along Wightman Fork Creek, is the sagging main pump house. Above the pump house stands a two-story wood-frame structure that looks like a dormitory. North of the road stand almost twenty buildings—cabins, pump houses, and outhouses. About a half dozen are partially or completely collapsed, but most are under roof.

When You Go
Summitville is 64 miles southeast of Creede and 27 miles southwest of Del Norte. To reach Summitville, head west from Del Norte on U.S. 160 for .4 of a mile to Pinos Creek Road (Road 14). Turn south and continue until a junction with Road 330 almost 18 miles from Del Norte. Turn right on 330. In another 1.5 miles, 330 goes left to Summitville. In good weather, a passenger car will suffice, but I recommend a truck.

Summitville's main pump house is, unfortunately, slowly sagging toward the horizontal. The building is well worth resurrecting because of one unusual feature—its "chimney" is actually a passageway so the pump house could be entered when winter snow covered the normal entrance.

Chapter Ten

SILVERTON GHOSTS

Left: *Silverton's depot is not utilized by the Durango & Silverton Railroad, but it stands trackside with a wagon ready for service.*

Above: *Ouray was the last stagecoach stop before entering the rugged San Juan Mountains and an important supply point for miners. The store of Gordon Kimball grossed more than $200,000 annually by selling prospecting supplies during the 1880s. This photo was taken in 1884. (Photo by Frank Kuykendall. Courtesy of the Ted Kierscey Photo Collection.)*

The San Juan Mountains are some of the most splendid in Colorado. Although they lack the proliferation of "Fourteeners" the Rockies can claim (of fifty-three fourteen-thousand-foot peaks in Colorado, only thirteen are found in the San Juans), these mountains have a drama, a spectacle, that is unique in the state.

Perched near the San Juan's pinnacles and nestled in its valleys are some of Colorado's most beautiful mining camps, including two in this chapter, Silverton and Ouray. Near both are true ghost towns in breathtaking settings.

The person who connected virtually every site listed in this and the next chapter was Otto Mears. He came to the United States a Russian orphan in 1850 at age ten, and a year later he was part of the California Gold Rush. A small man with towering energy, Mears later served in the Civil War, fought Indians under Kit Carson, and learned to speak the language of the Ute Indians fluently. In Colorado, he became known as the "Pathfinder of the San Juans" for his ability to create roads where others could not.

Mears was a friend of Ute Chief Ouray, for whom the town is named, and was instrumental in the signing of the 1873 Brunot Treaty, which opened up former Ute land to settlers.

Some of Mears's famous routes include a toll road from the San Luis Valley to Leadville, from Saguache to Lake City, and from Dallas (north of Ouray) to Telluride. His magnum opus was the incredible "Rainbow Route" from Ouray to Red Mountain; this route was a precursor to the famous "Million Dollar Highway," which still leaves tourists gasping with its hairpin turns, narrow curves, and steep drop-offs. Some muleskinners complained that Mears gave his roads turns so tight that a jackass needed a hinge in its middle to negotiate them.

Mears was a railroad builder as well. His first routes extended from Silverton to nearby mining camps. A more ambitious effort, the Rio Grande Southern, linked Durango to Ridgway, a town north of Ouray.

Silverton

Among the first prospectors to reach the San Juan Mountains was a party led by Captain Charles Baker in 1860, lured by his glowing accounts. Actual results were so meager that his disgruntled

A lone woman traverses Otto Mears's toll road between Ouray and Red Mountain in 1892. As precipitous as this section appears, even more breathtaking dropoffs occur nearer Ouray. (Photo by Keystone View Company. Courtesy of the Ted Kierscey Photo Collection.)

followers considered lynching him.

The area's isolation hindered exploration, but continued prospecting efforts in the 1870s brought pressure upon the federal government to "adjust" a treaty with the Ute Indians, essentially forcing them to give up their territory in the San Juans in an 1873 agreement known as the Brunot Treaty.

Two years later, a small community named Baker's Park was established in a lovely valley surrounded by silver-bearing mountains. The town was carefully platted and featured wide main streets to facilitate wagon traffic. The post office was granted to Silverton, likely a shortened version of "Silvertown." However, an apocryphal story claims the town got its name when a miner cried out that although they had no gold, they had "silver by the ton."

Transportation of even the richest ore created considerable obstacles for miners, because ore had to be packed out, transferred to wagons at the first road, and freighted to the nearest railhead, which originally was Pueblo. The arrival of the Denver & Rio Grande from Durango in 1882 alleviated that difficulty, cutting transportation costs

Silver ore may be less spectacular in appearance than gold, but it was primarily silver that fueled Colorado's early prosperity.

130

Old meets new: Silverton became dependent upon the Denver & Rio Grande Railroad from Durango for supplies. Mines near Silverton, however, still relied upon pack trains. Here burros and mules, some loaded and others still waiting, stand at a mining supply store across the street from the depot. (Photo by James M. Davis. Courtesy of the Ted Kierscey Photo Collection.)

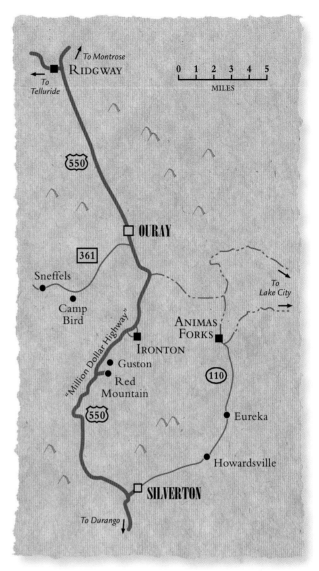

by 80 percent. Silverton's isolation was over—as long as the rails were clear. Snowslides in 1884, for example, forced snowbound citizens to scrape down to their last bits of food as they endured for seventy-three days before a train could get through. The link south to Durango remained the community's lifeline.

In addition to food, the railroad could bring in everything that makes a camp into a town. Silverton's Greene Street became an elegant thoroughfare, highlighted by the three-story brick Grand (later Grand Imperial) Hotel. Other commercial buildings vied for attention with attractive cornices and elaborate facades. Silverton never suffered a major fire, so the fine buildings remain intact today.

One block east stood Blair Street, so notorious for its saloons and brothels that residents at either end called their sections "Empire Street," to avoid being tainted by association.

The Silver Crash of 1893 dealt a blow to Silverton, but by 1897 half the ore production was for gold, followed by silver, lead, and copper. Output reached its zenith between 1900 and 1912 and continued until World War II.

The new gold arrived after World War II when the

Denver & Rio Grande's spectacular railroad began to attract tourists. Now called the Durango & Silverton Narrow Gauge, the train brings about two hundred thousand people to Silverton every year. (For more information, see chapter eleven's Durango entry.)

Walking and Driving Around Silverton

Silverton's stores offer a free visitors' guide that includes a walking tour.

An appropriate place to begin a tour is the San Juan County Museum, located at the north end of town. The museum is housed in the 1902 county jail, and much original equipment remains. The first floor features the sheriff's office and family quarters, the kitchen, and the women's cell. Men's cells are on the second floor, along with a door that once belonged to the jail at Animas Forks.

The Mayflower Mill and Old Hundred Mine Tours

Not far from Silverton are the best mill and mine tours I took in Colorado. To reach the Mayflower Mill and the Old Hundred Mine, drive to the north end of Silverton on Greene Street, turn right at the junction, and proceed northeast 1.9 miles to the Mayflower Mill. The Old Hundred is a half mile east of Howardsville (see following entry), which is two miles beyond the Mayflower Mill. Signs clearly mark the way to both attractions.

Mine tours should be enjoyable for almost everybody, because they are exciting and seem almost adventurous. Mills are different. I think you must want to know how a mill works, because a good mill tour will provide considerable information. I found the Mayflower Mill Tour fascinating.

Our guide, a ten-year mill employee, was informative and knowledgeable. As we walked through the mill, she told us, without unnecessarily elaborate explanations, how crude rocks were reduced to finished amalgam. The mill, incidentally, is intact, in sharp contrast to the Argo Mill in Idaho Springs (see chapter two).

The Old Hundred Mine Tour is excellent for a number of reasons. First, the train ride in, about seventeen hundred feet, is short enough not to be monotonous. Second, you explore several areas featuring different mining operations and equipment. Third, some of that equipment is actually operational; two drills and a mucker are fired up for just long enough to demonstrate that the mine certainly wasn't the silent place it is now. Finally, our tour guide was marvelous. A former miner, he could have been a siding salesman, so enthusiastic and entertaining was his pitch.

A short, beautiful side trip begins below the Mayflower Mill and crosses the Animas River. In only 1.5 miles, you follow a road toward the Mayflower Mine. You will frequently be near the towers that supported a tramway, which operated from 1930 until 1963 and transported ore from that mine to the Mayflower Mill. On occasion, you will pass beneath the buckets suspended overhead. At road's end, you will be creekside in magnificent Arrastra Gulch, looking up toward the mine itself.

Silverton's Hillside Cemetery looks down upon the picturesque town and has a sweeping view of the mountains surrounding the valley.

On your way downtown, visit the 1906 San Juan County Courthouse next door to the museum. Built in a cruciform configuration, its elaborate halls dramatically lead to a single central spot—a simple drinking fountain.

South of the courthouse on Greene is the 1902 Wyman Hotel, now a bed and breakfast. Across the street is the handsome 1908 town hall, gutted by a 1992 fire but beautifully restored by 1995. When you venture inside to see its graceful staircases, you will be amazed that skeptics considered the building beyond saving after the fire.

For the next four blocks heading south from the town hall, virtually every building on the west side of Greene dates back to the nineteenth century, as do many on the east side. Even newer buildings look authentic. Your visitors' guide will give you information on individual buildings.

Other commercial structures are found one block east of Greene on the once-notorious Blair Street. Notice the 1883 jail at the corner of Thirteenth and Blair. It was constructed by laying boards flat and stacking them log-cabin style on top of each other for strength. Examining this jail will help you better picture the remnants of similarly constructed jails at Animas Forks and Red Mountain.

One block west of Greene is Reese, where you will find many attractive residences. In that same area are the school, Carnegie Library, and three churches.

To reach Silverton's Hillside Cemetery, go north on Greene to a junction of roads. Take the north road and turn right at the first opportunity.

The oldest graves are to your left, past a small block shed near a fence. There you will find an unusual marker for Alfred Moyle, who died in 1888 at eight years. The stone features a child reclining on a blanket, with a clam shell spreading out protectively over him. Nearby is the cemetery's first burial plot, the 1875 grave of Rachel E. Farrow, along with the earliest headstone, for James Briggs, who died in a snowslide in 1878.

Three other interesting headstones are for William Henry Richards, who died in an 1889 Yankee Girl mining accident; for John Herbert, buried next to Richards, "accidentally hurt at Robinson Mine, Red Mountain," in 1890; and for Lewis Owen, next to Herbert, who died at the Yankee Girl in 1892.

When You Go
Silverton is 49 miles north of Durango and 25 miles south of Ouray on U.S. 550.

It is difficult to imagine today, but Howardsville was an early rival to Silverton.

Howardsville and Eureka

Howardsville and Eureka, along with Animas Forks beyond, offer a view into the varied states of true ghost towns. The first two have virtually vanished, but preservation efforts are alive at the third.

Howardsville
Howardsville was named either for a Lieutenant Howard of the Charles Baker Party or for prospector-miner George W. Howard, who built a cabin there in 1872. When the Hayden Geological Survey Party saw Howardsville in August 1874, they noted that the town had a post office, assay office, butcher shop, general store, and a cobbler's shop.

Howardsville features the tram terminus of the Little Nation Mine. Also at the site are a log cabin, a general store open for business, one frame residence, and the remodeled, updated Pride of the West Mill. The main attraction is the Old Hundred Mine Tour, located a half-mile east. (See page 132.)

Eureka
Eureka once had two thousand citizens. That fact alone is enough to make one pause at its scant ruins today.

Eureka became the milling center for the fabulously rich Sunnyside Mine, discovered in 1873, which is located almost a mile northwest of the townsite on the other side of Eureka Mountain. An extension of the Sunnyside vein, the Gold Prince Mine, featured ore melt

A new roof has been added to the Little Nation tram terminus at Howardsville to protect the historic relic. Ore from the Little Nation Mine was transported by the tramway to this building and then taken to the mill for processing.

On the western hillside are remnants of the Sunnyside mills. The smaller foundations on the left were for the earlier mill.

North of town .3 of a mile on the way to Animas Forks is a turnoff to an old three-story, wood-frame boarding house. Also along the route are cabin foundations and abandoned mines, along with some log cribbing. This log cribbing is all that remains of snowsheds built by Otto Mears in a futile attempt to protect his railroad from avalanches.

When You Go

From Silverton, drive north on Greene Street (State Route 110) and turn right when it divides. Howardsville is 3.9 miles northeast. Eureka is 3.7 miles north of Howardsville.

Animas Forks

A bit disappointed with the remains at Howardsville and Eureka? Along with remarkable scenery, Animas Forks makes the drive northeast from Silverton well worth while.

Personally, I will always have a special fondness for Animas Forks, given a somewhat adventurous trip I once made there. In late July 1989, several companions and I rode mountain bikes from Lake City to Silverton. At Cinnamon Pass we hit

that was 70 percent gold, 20 percent silver, and 10 percent lead.

Eureka's fortunes rose and fell with the Sunnyside mills. When the original mill was replaced by a larger one, the town prospered. When that mill burned, Eureka struggled. The new mill was rebuilt and operated from 1914 until 1938, when Eureka finally folded. Many buildings were moved elsewhere, with most going to Silverton. The tracks of Otto Mears's Silverton Northern Railway, which had hauled ore from Howardsville, Eureka, and Animas Forks, were taken up in 1942, the year the post office closed.

At the Eureka townsite today are evidence of foundations and basements, one log cabin, and a restored water tank, which later was modified to become a firehouse and jail.

a lightning-filled sleet storm and practically slid down to Animas Forks, where we found shelter and huddled together for warmth.

Animas Forks was founded in 1873 when prospectors built log cabins near their claims. Because three rivers met nearby, the camp was called Three Forks or Forks of the Animas. The name was simplified to Animas Forks by the U.S. Postal Service when a post office was granted in 1875.

At almost 11,200 feet, the town suffered from the elevation's severe winters. Most of the miners would retreat in the fall and return the following spring. The hearty few who stayed were subjected to avalanches and isolation. In 1884, the year Silverton endured ten weeks without relief supplies, Animas Forks was snowbound for twenty-three days. Provisions would have come from Silverton, which had none to spare.

Animas Forks emptied in 1891 as mining declined. A brief resurgence occurred in 1904 with the construction of the Gold Prince Mill, which was connected to its mine by a 2.4-mile tramway. That mill caused Otto Mears to extend his Silverton Northern Railway from Eureka to Animas Forks, further raising expectations for the town. But the mill closed in 1910, and Animas Forks lost its post office in 1915. In 1917, the mill was largely dismantled for use at Eureka's Sunnyside Mill.

At this writing, ten buildings stand completely or partially under roof around the townsite. As you cross the Animas Forks River entering town, foundations of the Gold Prince Mill will be on your right.

A brochure available at the site describes most of the other structures, among them the unusual jail. The jail is one of four in the area built using the same construction method—boards laid flat and stacked log-cabin style, so the structure has a stockade's strength. Others stand in Silverton, Red Mountain, and Telluride. The door to this one is now housed in the museum in Silverton.

When You Go

Animas Forks is 4.2 miles north of Eureka and 12 miles northeast of downtown Silverton on State Route 110.

Right, top: *The Columbus Mill at Animas Forks processed ore from the nearby Columbus Mine, which produced zinc until about 1915. In the background are several residences of Animas Forks, including the Duncan house.*

Right, bottom: *One of Colorado's more photographed ghost town buildings is the 1879 William Duncan home with its dramatic bay window.*

Red Mountain, Guston, and Ironton

These three minor ghost towns combine to make one interesting, extended ghost town site along the Million Dollar Highway.

Red Mountain

The town of Red Mountain lies beneath three peaks—Red Mountain numbers 1, 2, and 3. These three mountains gave their name to two towns. The first was Red Mountain City, located south of Red Mountain Pass. Its larger rival was Red Mountain Town, located slightly east of the pass. The latter boomed when the National Belle Mine was discovered in 1882. A post office opened in 1883, and the population soared to about a thousand. Red Mountain City faded to obscurity, and Red Mountain Town became the only Red Mountain.

Otto Mears constructed a road to Red Mountain from Ouray in 1883, and five years later his railroad reached the site from Silverton. The town was so narrow that the depot was constructed inside the track's wye. The many saloons served triple duty as theaters and courtrooms in a town known for its raucous behavior.

The 1893 Silver Crash paralyzed the town, and by 1896 the population had fallen to a few dozen. Mining resumed in 1901, but the bonanza was over.

At Red Mountain Pass today are the remains of the Longfellow Mine, including a wood frame dormitory with its stove still inside. The Longfellow is east of the highway near milepost eighty.

North of the Red Mountain Pass signpost .3 of a mile is the turnoff to Red Mountain. The townsite, a half mile east of the highway, features the headframe of the National Belle Mine, one adjacent building under roof, and one collapsed structure. Across Red Mountain Creek is what no doubt was the jail, constructed like the jail buildings in Silverton and Animas Forks.

When you return to the highway, you have a one-mile drive north before coming to the Idarado milling complex, which operated until 1978. At a hairpin turn you will see several residences and what appears to be a boarding house. More than ninety miles of tunnels connect the Idarado complex to Pandora, near Telluride. The Idarado site is now a major reclamation project.

Guston

Guston was founded in 1881 and named for a mine that was one of the district's biggest producers. But the true bonanza of the area was the Yankee Girl, discovered by John Robinson. The town that grew near the mines included a church founded by Reverand William Davis, who had been sent from Denver to Red Mountain to

Left: The headframe of the National Belle mine, a major producer at Red Mountain, stands at the townsite.

Below: The now almost-vanished Red Mountain Town, with its schoolhouse in the right foreground, is pictured here in 1888. In 1892, the town was virtually destroyed by fire. At the hotel, people furiously piled everything from billiard tables and roulette wheels to lamps and quilts out of harm's way. When the wind changed, the effort proved fruitless. (Courtesy of the Ted Kierscey Photo Collection.)

Miners pose at the Yankee Girl Mine at Guston in 1888. Note the decimation of the surrounding forest in this photo. Today's trees at Guston, as at most Colorado mining camps, are mostly secondary growth. (Photo by Griffith and Griffith. Courtesy of the Ted Kierscey Photo Collection.)

The Yankee Girl boarding house at Guston has five rooms on the first floor. The second floor can be reached only by a rickety outdoor stairway.

establish a Congregational church. Red Mountain, however, showed no interest, so Davis went to Guston, where people were more receptive. Davis's daughter recalled that on the same day the church was dedicated in 1892, a terrible fire devoured Red Mountain (perhaps the one that consumed billiard tables and roulette wheels). At least one Red Mountain resident saw the two events as divinely connected.

When author Muriel Sibell Wolle first visited Guston before World War II, the church was still standing, but on subsequent trips she saw its decline and disappearance.

Guston has essentially vanished. The Yankee Girl Mine's hoist house still stands north of the townsite, and the principal attraction is the Yankee Girl boarding house, a large, two-story wooden structure that can be seen south of the highway and below the hoist house. The turnoff to the boarding house is 1.8 miles northeast of the Idarado Mill gate (3.4 miles from Red Mountain Pass). Looking at the building, I thought of William Henry Richards and Lewis Owen, who died at the Yankee Girl and are buried at Silverton's Hillside Cemetery, and wondered which rooms were theirs.

Ironton

Ironton yields more ghost town treasures than the previous two sites combined. Located northeast of Guston, it can be reached by driving from the Yankee Girl turnoff for 1.4 miles along U.S. 550 toward Ouray. In about a mile you will see a roofed cabin on the left side of the

road, along with a chute, adit, and mining debris. These are the remains of the Larson Brothers Mine. (Bob Larson, the last Ironton resident, died in 1967.)

Beyond those remnants .2 of a mile, turn right near a huge tailings pile. Head back, parallel to the highway, along the base of the tailings. When the road starts to curl around to the right, take a lesser road to the left that parallels the creek. In .7 of a mile you will come to the remains of Ironton.

Ironton came into existence in 1882 when Guston and Red Mountain boomed. Named for the silver-iron ore common in the district, Ironton received its post office in 1883, the same year Otto Mears's road from Ouray reached Red Mountain. When Mears's railroad was completed from Silverton to Ironton, the town became an important shipping point. Goods were transferred there between railroad and freight wagons, because the route from Ironton to Ouray was too steep for a railroad, even for one constructed by Otto Mears.

Ironton depended upon the fortunes of nearby mines, which failed after the turn of the century. Ironton lost its post office in 1920 and was dead when the railroad tracks were salvaged in 1926. A few homes were renovated when the Idarado Mill was operating.

Today Ironton is hidden from the highway, which probably accounts for its good condition. You will find a wood and tin building in ruins, a hewn-log structure with a lumber false front, four outbuildings, and a photogenic, two-story frame white house with a two-story bay window. In this home I saw a notice about preserving ghost towns that so impressed me that I included it in my message to the reader at the beginning of this book. Beyond that residence are two more two-story homes, the last featuring wainscoting in the kitchen-dining area.

Remember that these buildings are tangible, but fragile remnants of Colorado's history. Because they are so hidden, they are more vulnerable than many in this book.

Three monuments stand on the roadside between Ironton and Ouray. The first two are 2.5 miles from the Ironton turnoff. The first memorializes three maintenance workers who died trying to keep this road open. The second is for Reverand Martin Hudson and his two daughters, who died in an avalanche in 1963. Beyond those memorials .4 of a mile is one to "pathfinder" Otto Mears.

When You Go

Red Mountain is 10 miles north of Silverton and 13 miles south of Ouray on U.S. 550. See the text for directions to Guston and Ironton.

Ouray

When fishing buddies A. J. Staley and Logan Whitlock found gold lodes along the Uncompahgre River in July 1875, they named their claims the Trout and the Fisherman. A month later, Gus Begole and Jack Eckles found the Mineral Farm claim, so named because of its rows of parallel veins. Prospectors then swarmed in.

The camp at the end of a box canyon was originally called Uncompahgre City. ("Uncompahgre" is a spelling variation of the Ute word "Ancapagari," meaning "Red Lake," which was a description of the bad-tasting, red-colored water near the river's source.) The name was soon changed to Ouray in honor of Tabequache Ute Chief Ouray, who was highly respected by white men for his role in opening the San Juans for exploration.

Chief Ouray was the official spokesman of the entire Ute tribe in the eyes of the U.S. government, though many Ute factions did not recognize his authority. He nevertheless brokered compromises and calmed potentially violent confrontations, because he believed that fighting white soldiers was ultimately futile. Born in 1833, he died in 1880, shortly before the exodus of virtually all Utes from Colorado to Utah, a sight that no doubt would have saddened, but not surprised, him.

Because of the area's wicked winters, the town of Ouray suffered early from its isolation and was routinely short of supplies, even necessities. Help came from Pathfinder Otto Mears, who in 1881 built a road from Dallas, twelve miles north of Ouray, over Dallas Divide to Telluride. His second road led up to the Virginius Mine on Mount Sneffels. His third and most famous extended to Red Mountain along what later became the Million Dollar Highway. The first road improved the reliability of supplies. The other two allowed the mines at Sneffels (and, later, Camp Bird) and Red Mountain to ship huge quantities of lower-grade ore, vastly increasing the wealth of the entire district—including the ultimate supply point, Ouray. When a branch of the Denver & Rio Grande Railroad reached Ouray from Montrose in 1887, profits soared.

The Silver Crash of 1893 hurt Ouray, but enough gold was shipped along with silver that the town soon recovered, especially after the monstrous gold discovery at Camp Bird in 1895 (see following entry).

Walking and Driving Around Ouray

Free guides for touring Ouray are available in many places, including the Ouray County Museum, located at 420 Sixth Avenue. Formerly St. Joseph's Hospital, it was built in 1887 and operated until 1964 under the Catholic Sisters of Mercy. Among the interesting artifacts in the museum is Chief Ouray's headdress and a replica of the Hope Diamond, once owned by Evalyn Walsh McLean of Camp Bird (see following entry). An extensive mineral display is in the basement. The museum's second floor features rooms faithful to their original function—an operating room, a patient's room, and a doctor's office.

Several outstanding government and commercial buildings, along with many lovely residences, stand in Ouray. Here's the route I suggest taking. Start on Main Street and Seventh Avenue. Head east on Seventh to view the 1895 Story House at the northwest corner of Seventh and Fourth Streets. Turn right on Fourth and proceed to the 1888 Ouray County Courthouse with its mansard-roofed cupola. Beyond it is the lovely 1888 Ashley House at 505 Fourth Street and the small but delightful 1880s Hurlburt House at 445 Fourth Street. On the northwest corner of Fourth and Third Avenue stands the elegant 1901 Tanner House.

Turn west on Third Avenue and return to Main Street. Along Main are some of Colorado's most delightful commercial buildings, among them the handsome 1904 Elks Lodge at 421 Main, featuring an elegant corner turret, and the 1886 Beaumont Hotel with its ornate multiple facades at Main and Fifth Avenue. On Sixth Avenue east of Main is city hall, built in 1901 to resemble Independence Hall in Philadelphia. The structure burned in 1950 but was restored in 1988.

The three-story, wood-frame, 1891 Western Hotel, west of the main business district at Second Street and Seventh Avenue, features elaborate exterior wood detailing.

Ouray, located at the end of a box canyon, is often referred to as "Switzerland of the United States."

Ouray's Beaumont Hotel was once one of Colorado's premier hostelries. More than one attempt has been made to resurrect the 1886 building, but at this writing it remains vacant and deteriorating.

One sight not to miss in Ouray is Box Canyon Falls, south of town on the road to Camp Bird. There Canyon Creek plummets 285 feet through a narrow cleft in an astonishing performance of power and sound.

The Ouray Cemetery is located 5.5 miles north of Ouray on U.S. 550 in a serene, lovely setting, with red cliffs serving as a backdrop. An unusual feature of the cemetery is found in the Elks Rest section. All the head-

Bachelor-Syracuse Mine Tour

I found this mine tour quite enjoyable, principally because of our pleasant and informative guide, a former Bachelor-Syracuse miner. There were two shortcomings, however. For one, the mine train takes quite a while to go three thousand feet into the mine. For another, the tour stays in one spot. Although the guide gave an excellent presentation on mining methods, standing in one place can be tiring, especially for children. Nevertheless, I certainly recommend the tour. (Even more highly recommended, however, is the Old Hundred Mine Tour, near Silverton.)

To visit the Bachelor-Syracuse, go two miles north from Ouray to County Road 14, where signs lead you 1.4 miles to the mine.

stones are identical and in chronological order from 1907 until 1938.

When You Go

Ouray is 25 miles north of Silverton and 10 miles south of Ridgway on U.S. 550.

Camp Bird and Sneffels

Camp Bird

Camp Bird came to fame in 1895, when Irishman Thomas Walsh sent prospector Andy Richardson to look for ores to use for flux in Walsh's Silverton smelter. The result was not flux but rather an astounding gold strike at the Gertrude, a claim abandoned in the 1870s. Walsh purchased numerous other claims but also let Richardson stake his own. Richardson named his Camp Bird, a miner's name for the Canada or gray jay, a bird also known as the "Camp Robber" for its habit of stealing food or even objects. Walsh called the consolidated claims Camp Bird as well.

Miners at Camp Bird enjoyed luxuries unheard of in other company towns, except perhaps Redstone (see chapter five). They dined on china plates, read provided magazines under electric lights, and bathed in porcelain tubs in their huge boarding house.

Walsh became fabulously wealthy, buying a mansion in Washington, D.C. and entering his wife and daughter Evalyn into eastern society. Evalyn married *Washington Post* heir Edward McLean, with each family contributing $100,000 to their honeymoon spending money.

Above: This frame building at the Torpedo-Eclipse Mine at Sneffels appears to have once been part of a milling operation. However, it has an unstable second floor, so do not enter it.

Left: Ruins of the Atlas Stamp Mill stand a half mile beyond Sneffels. At the left rear are the remnants of part of the stamping operation that once crushed the ore, although the stamps themselves are gone.

Walsh sold the Camp Bird Mine in 1902 for $5.2 million, giving his employees bonuses of as much as $5,000 each. The mine totaled more than $47 million in production by the time it shut down in 1978.

Evalyn Walsh McLean, incidentally, became the owner of the Hope Diamond. She purchased it despite its famous curse and wore it constantly—no picture was taken of her without it.

Today, Camp Bird is posted against trespassing. Two outstanding buildings, the mine office and the mine manager's house (featuring a handsome turret), are only partially visible from public vantage points.

Sneffels

Sneffels, founded in 1875 by Silverton prospectors, predates Camp Bird. It was named for "Fourteener" Mount Sneffels, which was named by a Hayden Survey Party member in 1874. One geologist apparently thought Blue Lake Basin resembled a crater described in Jules Verne's 1864 novel *Journey to the Center of the Earth*. Another geologist then gave the peak above the basin the name Sneffels, for the mountain in the same novel.

The town's Wheel of Fortune Mine was an early success, followed by others such as the Yankee Boy and the Revenue. The greatest mine of them all, however, was the Virginius, especially after the $600,000 Revenue Tunnel was bored two miles into Mount Sneffels. A miner boasted in 1897, "No man alive today will see the supply exhausted." He was right; at today's value, more than $1 billion in gold and silver was extracted before the mine closed.

At Sneffels today are remnants of the Revenue-Virginius operation, including four old structures, one of which is under roof with its windows boarded. Above and behind them stand later tin buildings. North of the road are two buildings and an adit covered by a large iron grating.

The face of the Sneffels area may change. An Idaho mining company announced in September 1998 that it intends to have the Revenue-Virginius producing silver by the year 2000.

When You Go

To reach Camp Bird and Sneffels, head south from Ouray on U.S. 550. In .6 of a mile, turn south onto Road 361, a twisting, steep mountain road. Camp Bird is 4.6 miles from the highway. I recommend a high-clearance vehicle, although I saw a passenger car at Sneffels, which is 1.5 miles west of Camp Bird.

Ridgway

Ridgway was born when Otto Mears created a junction for his Rio Grande Southern Railroad to link with the Montrose-to-Ouray branch of the Denver & Rio Grande. The Rio Grande Southern extended from Ridgway to Telluride and Durango. Originally called Magentie, the town soon chose Ridgway in honor of Robert M. Ridgway, superintendent of the Denver & Rio Grande and head of the construction company that built Mears's railroad. The town was incorporated in 1890 and became the headquarters of the Rio Grande Southern a year later, with rail yards and repair shops adjacent to the growing town.

When the 1893 Silver Crash forced the Rio Grande Southern into receivership, the Denver & Rio Grande temporarily assumed operations of the line. The Great Depression also hit Ridgway hard, and many bank customers lost their savings in 1931 when their bank's president illegally invested their money and securities. The town's fortunes continued to decline, as the Rio Grande Southern never recovered fully from the crash of 1893. Despite creative efforts to keep it afloat (see the Dolores entry in chapter eleven), the route ceased operation in 1951.

As you enter Ridgway on State Route 62 from U.S. 550, the first historic building is along Railroad Avenue, west of the river; this attractive residence north of the highway was once the Denver & Rio Grande depot.

A pleasant feature of Ridgway is Hartwell Park, named for the director of the Rio Grande Southern. The park appeared in the films *True Grit* and *How the West was Won*. Facing the park is the firehouse, a stone structure with a wooden and brick facade and a jaunty bell tower. (The tower is not original to the building; it was added for *True Grit*.) The stone jail is directly behind it. Around the corner along Clinton Street stands the 1890 bank building, along with several other older structures, including the 1915 Sherbino Block and Theater. If you continue west on Clinton, you will see several attractive residences, including the Stanwood-Carmichael home. Located on the northwest corner of Clinton and Laura, it is a brick house with the front door on the diagonal.

Another interesting building is the 1891 Herran House, a two-story brick building at 162 North Cora, which is unusual because it is a commercial building in front, but a residence in back. The Rasmussen Home on the northwest corner of Charlotte and Hyde is also unusual, with its pressed-tin sheathing. A short time spent crisscrossing the streets of Ridgway will yield other architecturally diverse buildings.

To reach Ridgway's Dallas Park Cemetery, drive west from town 2.5 miles on State Route 62.

When You Go

Ridgway is 10 miles north of downtown Ouray on U.S. 550.

Chapter Eleven

DURANGO GHOSTS

Left: *A shack leans precariously at Alta, one of Colorado's most picturesque ghost towns. Behind is the much sturdier two-story boardinghouse for single miners.*

Above: *The look and spirit of the 1906 Animas City School have been preserved by the La Plata County Historical Society at the Animas Museum in Durango. Located in the town's original school house, the museum features this restored first-floor classroom. The building's second floor holds displays on everything from the history of the town fire fighters to lessons in saddle making.*

Durango and Telluride are justly popular tourist destinations; one has the exciting Durango-to-Silverton railroad, the other has skiing and scenery. But both also played an important role in southwestern Colorado's mining history and feature numerous historic attractions. This chapter also offers appealing sites such as the semi–ghost town of Rico, the true ghost of Alta, and the ruins of the Tomboy Mine, all of which offer spectacular vistas of the San Juan Mountains. The chapter essentially follows the route of Otto Mears's Rio Grande Southern Railroad from Durango to Telluride, with a couple of side trips along the way.

Durango

Durango was an important cog in the mining machinery of the 1880s, serving as the rail hub and smelting site for San Juan silver and gold strikes. With nearby farmlands and coal fields, Durango ensured the food and fuel supply of countless miners and mines.

Named for a Mexican city, Durango was created in 1880 when Animas City, founded four years earlier, balked at concessions requested by the Denver & Rio Grande. The railroad simply established its own town two miles south. When tracks were extended past Animas City to Silverton, Animas City had been outflanked. Durango became the seat of La Plata County in 1881, while Animas City was relegated to living in Durango's shadow.

Durango became one of Colorado's four great smelter towns, along with Denver, Leadville, and Pueblo. The Silver Crash of 1893 and the subsequent depression caused Durango to evolve into an agricultural center, with smelting a lesser industry, by World War I.

Smelter operations closed in 1929 at the onset of the Great Depression, but mills were busy during World War II extracting vanadium and, secretly, uranium. Some of that uranium was used in the atomic bombs dropped on Hiroshima and Nagasaki. Uranium milling continued in Durango during the early stages of the Cold War; however, cleaning up the uranium tailings later cost taxpayers $15 million.

Walking and Driving Around Durango
Main Avenue is the center of activity in town. A free walking tour brochure is widely available. Two major attractions are the 1882 railroad depot, headquarters of the Durango &

Crucibles such as these were used to assay ore.

Silverton Narrow Gauge Railroad, and the elegant 1888 Strater Hotel, which once featured pianos in its most luxurious bedrooms. About two dozen other historic buildings line Main between Fifth and Twelfth Streets.

To see Durango's most attractive residences and churches, take a drive down Third Avenue, two blocks east of Main.

The Animas Museum of the La Plata County Historical Society, located one block west of Main and one block south of Thirty-second Street on the north end of Durango, is housed in the 1906 Animas City School. The first floor has a restored classroom, while the second floor features several informative displays, including an excellent photographic history of Durango's fire department.
When You Go
Durango is 49 miles south of Silverton on U.S. 550.

Mancos

Mancos was an agricultural center and later a railroad stop along the Rio Grande Southern. The town, named for the river flowing through it, received its post office in 1877. Otto Mears's railroad from Ridgway to Durango was completed in 1891, with Mancos as one of the last major stops before Durango.

Mancos's principal intersection is Main and Grand, the names indicating that early settlers might have had loftier plans for Mancos than what actually materialized for the town. On the southwest corner of that intersection is the restored 1905, two-story brick and stone Bauer Bank Building. West on Grand stands the 1910 Mancos Opera House, and farther on is the 1909 Mancos High School with its unusual bell tower. A sign indicates that it is Colorado's oldest high school in continuous use.

Two of the loveliest homes in Mancos are the 1890 Bauer House on Main at Bauer Avenue and the 1903 Wrightsman House on Bauer at Mesa. Both are now bed and breakfast inns.

Cedar Grove Cemetery is .7 of a mile south of Mancos. Take Main and follow it as it becomes Weber Road (County Road 41). Beyond that cemetery 1.4 miles is Weber Cemetery, a Mormon graveyard on private property.
When You Go
Mancos is 28 miles west of Durango on U.S. 160. The highway bypasses the business district, which is two blocks south.

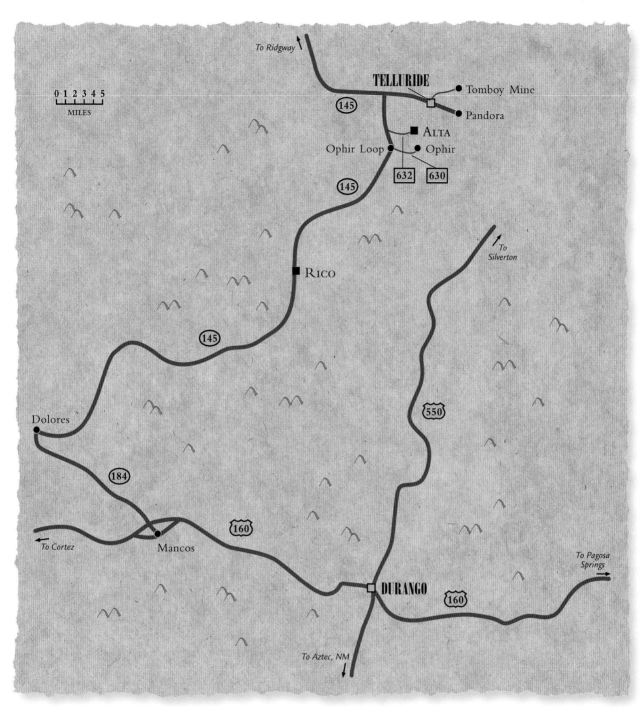

To Ridgway

TELLURIDE ● Tomboy Mine

(145) ● Pandora

■ ALTA

Ophir Loop ● ● Ophir

632 630

(145)

To Silverton

■ RICO

(145)

(550)

Dolores

(184)

To Cortez

(160)

Mancos

To Pagosa Springs

DURANGO (160)

To Aztec, NM

0 1 2 3 4 5
MILES

The San Juan Smelter, located at the base of Smelter Mountain on the south end of Durango, was in full operation when this photo was taken around 1894. The smelter was closed in 1930 and converted for use as a vanadium and uranium mill from World War II until 1963. The last buildings were demolished in 1987. Across the Animas River from the smelter site today is Durango's Gateway Park. (Courtesy of the La Plata County Historical Society.)

Durango & Silverton Narrow Gauge Railroad

People from all over the world come to ride this spectacular train, and so should you. You can choose a round-trip journey or a one-way with a bus return. If you have small children, you might prefer the latter. Otherwise, I recommend the nine-hour round trip. If you want to enjoy your day to the utmost, go first class in the 1880 Alamosa Parlor Car (no minors allowed, however). I confess that having taken the Alamosa twice, I'm spoiled.

The Durango & Silverton is not inexpensive, but the day's memories will be worth the cost. Reservations are strongly recommended. Whether you take the train or not, consider visiting the railroad's museum, where you can climb inside a caboose and a private business coach and even take the engineer's spot in the cab of a 1902 locomotive. An outdoor viewing area allows you to watch mechanics work locomotives in the roundhouse and, if you are lucky, to see a locomotive on the turntable.

Engine #42, which was built in 1887 and is no longer in service, stands adjacent to the Durango depot, the southern terminus of the Durango & Silverton Narrow Gauge Railroad. It currently resides inside the railroad's museum.

Dolores

Dolores was founded in 1891 as a stop along the Rio Grande Southern Railroad. Here the tracks crossed the Dolores River and entered Lost Canyon on the way to Mancos. Because the Rio Grande Southern was built to serve silver mines, the Silver Crash of 1893, a short two years after the railroad's completion, meant the railroad would always struggle to survive.

In 1931, the railway tried to tighten its belt by introducing the "Galloping Goose," which could traverse the line much more economically than a conventional train. The name came either from its noisy air horn or its appearance in action; according to an old railroad man, the "darned rig looks like an old goose a-flappin' and a-gallopin' down the track."

The eight "Geese" were variations on a common theme—each was part automobile and part freight car, driven by a powerful automobile engine. Later modifications to three Geese added a Wayne Bus body wedged between auto hood and freight car. The amalgamations looked gangly and ridiculous, but they worked. Even the Galloping Geese, however, couldn't keep the line open indefinitely, and the route was abandoned on New Year's Eve of 1951.

Galloping Goose #5 dwells next to a replica of the Rio Grande Southern depot in Dolores. The completely restored Goose now makes special runs on the Durango & Silverton and Cumbres & Toltec narrow-gauge railroads.

In Dolores today, Central Avenue, a block north of the highway, has most of the town's historic structures. These buildings include the Exon Mercantile and the 1892 Rio Grande Southern Hotel, along with several attractive homes east of downtown.

Along the highway is the Dolores Visitors' Center, a 1990s replica of the old train depot. In front stands a wonderful sight—Galloping Goose #5. When I first visited Dolores in the 1980s, the Goose was in a sad state, but by 1998 the noble machine had been completely restored by volunteers. It has a replacement engine, thanks to Knott's Berry Farm in southern California, which donated the one from their Goose #3.

In addition to the one in California, three surviving Geese reside at the Colorado Railroad Museum in Golden, while another sits in Telluride. (For a definitive—and extremely wry—history of the Geese, read Stanley Rhine's *Galloping Geese on the Rio Grande Southern*.)

When You Go
Dolores is 17 miles northwest of Mancos on State Route 184 and 12 miles northeast of Cortez on State Route 145.

Rico

If you want to visit Rico the semi–ghost town, do it soon. A mining company that owned large tracts of land around town has sold them to developers. A worried resident told me that "Rico might, God forbid, become another Telluride."

Prospectors worked the streams and hills around Rico as early as 1866, but it wasn't until 1876 that they formed the Pioneer Mining District. Two years later, R. C. Darling found silver, lead, zinc, and copper near the confluence of the Dolores River and Silver Creek and staked the Atlantic Cable claim.

Rico boomed in 1879, when silver was found on Blackhawk and Telescope mountains and other hills in the area.

Tents and cabins were erected in a haphazard flurry of excitement, leading the *Ouray Times* to comment, "The place impresses one as having gotten there before it was sent for." The new community was named Rico (Spanish for "rich").

In 1881, Rico became the seat of newly created Dolores County. Six years later, David Swickhimer located the Enterprise Mine in the area but lacked the capital to exploit it. His wife Laura invested a dollar on a lottery ticket, and it paid $5,000, which she insisted they use for the mine. Four years later, they sold the Enterprise for $1.25 million. Unfortunately, they invested that money unwisely, he in banking and she in real estate, and ended back where they started—except divorced.

The 1893 Silver Crash ended the bonanza times, though mining continued sporadically into the next century. A modest rebirth in 1926 brought better times to Rico, but the best days were over. The town named for its great mineral riches suffered a stinging defeat in 1941 when the county seat moved to Dove Creek, "Pinto Bean Capital of the World."

Coming from Dolores, you will see Rico's cemeteries on both sides of the road before you enter the town. Many graves are for people of German descent and at least one grave is inscribed in Italian. One touching double grave is for sisters Ina and Fannie Burchardt, who were born a year and a half apart but died on consecutive days in 1890.

As you enter Rico, on the east side the highway is the Rico Hotel. Built around 1925, it originally served as a miners' bunkhouse. Down the street is the Rohde Inn, featuring an unusual oriel window.

The elementary school is now the Rico Center, kept open by volunteer help in hopes it will reopen as a school; at this writing, children are bused seventy-two miles round-trip daily to Dolores to attend school.

Other historic downtown structures include the native-stone Rico State Bank Building (where Swickhimer lost his money paying off depositors), the brick Rico Masonic Lodge, and the 1892 cut-sandstone Dey Building.

East of the highway is the town's premier structure, the former Dolores County Courthouse. An attractive

The 1892 Dolores County Courthouse (now the town hall and library) and the 1891 Rico Community Church flank a well-kept wood-frame home in Rico.

community church, a brick commercial building, and several residences stand nearby.

On your way to Telluride, stop at Lizard Head Pass for information on the rail yards that once stood there. North of the pass 1.4 miles, an old railroad car reminds travelers that this was once Rio Grande Southern territory.

When You Go

Rico is 36 miles northeast of Dolores and 27 miles southwest of Telluride on State Route 145.

Ophir and Ophir Loop

Ophir was a mining camp, while Ophir Loop owes its existence to the Rio Grande Southern Railroad.

The area's first claim was staked in 1875, but miners only drifted into the district until the discovery of the Osceola and Gold King claims in 1879.

The camp of about fifty miners was named for the site in the Old Testament from which gold was "fetched" and taken to King Solomon. This new Ophir had gold to fetch as well, with mines such as the Silver Bell, What Cheer, and the marvelously named Butterfly-Terrible steadily producing ore.

Winters were difficult in Ophir, with supplies and mail always doubtful. On December 23, 1883, mailcarrier Swan Nilson left Silverton, despite warnings from the postmaster, and headed over Ophir Pass. When he failed to arrive, Ophir citizens griped that Nilson had fled with their valuable Christmas mail. His brother drew another conclu-

sion and diligently searched for Swan's body, finally discovering it in a snowbank—with the secured mailbag—nearly two years later.

When Otto Mears's Rio Grande Southern Railroad came through in 1891, a curving, hundred-foot-high trestle was built two miles west of Ophir. A depot was erected and Ophir Loop was born.

Ophir Loop also featured a store, hotel, and the mill for the Butterfly-Terrible. In addition, it served as the lower terminus of a tramway from Alta, two miles away (see the following entry).

Ophir declined as ore bodies diminished. The 1940 census found two residents; the 1960 found none. That 1960 census taker, however, missed the mayor and sole resident Jim Noyes, who was off in Grand Junction.

Today, the side road off the highway immediately enters Ophir Loop. The first building on the left was likely the hotel or a boarding house. Another frame structure is beyond it, and on the right are the remnants of the Silver Bell Mine, noted as "active" on the 1955 topographic map.

Two years after that map was drawn, the highway was improved. To accommodate the road, the Rio Grande Southern depot, which then housed the Ophir post office and a store, was demolished.

The current post office is .6 of a mile east of the highway, and Ophir itself is 1.5 miles beyond the post office. Most of Ophir consists of newer buildings, but more than half a dozen appear to be of antiquity.

Left: *Fall colors surround a mine adit near Ophir. The rotting timbers, however, attest to the dangers of old mines.*

Below: *A whimsically painted ore train near Ophir Loop stands among leafless aspens in what was once Rio Grande Southern Railroad territory.*

The Ophir Cemetery offers an excellent view of Ophir Pass, the one Nilson died traversing. When the road through town turns toward the pass, go north into a residential area. The road veers to the east; the cemetery is north of the road.

Many graves are mere unmarked mounds, located both in a clearing and among aspens and blue spruce, which form a canopy over a carpet of maidenhair. Fewer than a dozen graves are marked, including an unusual cylindrical one for Pearl Marchand, who died in 1903. The marker for former mayor Jim Noyes (1879–1967) reads "Nebraska Pioneer, Colorado Goldminer."

When You Go
Ophir Loop is 16.5 miles northeast of Rico and 10.4 miles southwest of Telluride on State Route 145. Ophir is 2.1 miles east of Ophir Loop on Forest Service Road 630, the route over Ophir Pass.

Alta

Alta (Spanish for "high") was a company town for the Gold King Mine, discovered in 1878. Alta had a general store, an assay office, a school, miners' homes, and company offices. The town also became the upper terminus for a tram that extended almost two miles and dropped more than eighteen hundred feet to Ophir Loop, where a loading bin was located near the Rio Grande Southern depot.

The Alta-area mines produced into the 1940s under the ownership of the Silver Mountain Mining Company, but a fire in one of the shafts in 1945 effectively ended production.

When I first saw Alta in 1987, it was abandoned and deteriorating. Since then, efforts have begun to preserve and protect the buildings. The Alta I first saw, if left to the elements and vandals, would be in a sorry state today.

When you enter Alta, you will be at the bottom of the site, where water tumbles off old waste dumps. Nearby are two crumbling wooden structures and, as you turn toward the upper site, five more miners' shacks.

You will come to a good place to park on a flat spot above, where a roofless log building stands that served as

Lizard Head Peak is framed within the window of the old mine office and company store at Alta.

the mine office and a company store. Across the way is an impressive two-story boarding house, built in 1939. Behind you is an astonishing view of Lizard Head Peak, Wilson Peak, and Sunshine Mountain.

Up a low hill to the northwest are four more modern residences that housed mining officials. Other structures in one state of collapse or another complete a kind of circle around the open area. On my visit, the officials' houses were posted against entering, but not against approaching. Beyond the four was a fifth in shambles. One home, probably the mining superintendent's, has an attractive bay window that likely has a spectacular view.

From the waste dump you will see lots of mining debris—buckets, pipe, slabs of concrete, and a geared wheel. Northwest of the main site are six wooden foundations and a log cabin. The school once stood in this area, according to the 1955 topographic map.

When You Go
From Ophir Loop, drive 1.8 miles north on State Route 145 to the turnoff to Alta, Forest Service Road 632.

149

The townsite comes into view in 3.5 miles.

From Telluride, head west to State Route 145. Turn south on 145 and drive 5.2 miles to the turnoff marked for Alta Lakes (the lakes are one mile beyond the Alta townsite).

Telluride, Pandora, and the Tomboy Mine

Telluride

Telluride today is a famous skiing destination and the site of prestigious film and music festivals. Like Aspen, however, its roots are in mining.

In 1875, the Sheridan claim was staked high in Marshall Basin, three thousand feet above the San Miguel River's path through a narrow valley. Another claim, the Union, was staked adjacent to it. When J. B. Ingram investigated the claims, he found them to be oversized, so he fit his own claim, innocently named the Smuggler, within the original two. When the Smuggler and Union were eventually combined, they became enormously successful.

The town that grew along the San Miguel in 1878 was originally called Columbia, but by 1883 it was known

as Telluride, named for the chemical element tellurium, which, oddly, does not occur in the minerals in the district. Citizens, however, enjoyed warning others that, if you came to their wide-open town, it was "To-Hell-You-Ride!"

By the following year, Telluride had a thousand residents and was the seat of newly formed San Miguel County. A county seat, however, does not guarantee gentility, and in its early years Telluride was well known for its lawlessness, alcohol consumption, and red light district.

With the Silver Crash of 1893, Telluride temporarily came to a halt, but by the late 1890s rich gold deposits were located, and the boom was on again. As time went on, fierce labor confrontations, declining ore bodies, and finally the Great Depression made Telluride into a near ghost. By 1970, it had only 553 citizens, down from 2,446 in 1900. When Muriel Sibell Wolle visited Telluride in 1972, she knew that a ski development was planned, so she returned to see "the quiet mining town before 'progress' caught up with it."

Walking and Driving Around Telluride

Progress has certainly caught up with it, but like other rediscovered Colorado mining towns, Telluride still has considerable charm and plenty of history.

Telluride has its own widely available summer visitors' guide, which includes a map of town and its various historic buildings. You can refer to such a guide for a detailed tour, but here are some of my favorite stops.

Colorado Avenue, the main street through town, features many excellent buildings, including the 1887 San Miguel County Courthouse, at Oak Street. Take a gander (sorry) at Galloping Goose #4 nesting adjacent to the courthouse. The New Sheridan Hotel and Opera House is across Oak from the courthouse. Built in 1895, the Sheridan was one of Colorado's classiest hotels and featured the Continental Room, where diners used tableside phones to summon waiters.

A block north, on Columbia at Oak, is the lovely 1894 Davis House. At Pine and Galena, north of Columbia, stands one of the prettiest homes in Telluride, the Waggoner House. Banker Charles Waggoner became a hero during the stock market crash of 1929 when he devised a scheme to pay off his depositors at the expense of New York banks. He went to prison for three years, but he was revered locally.

Telluride's 1878 jail, like the ones at Silverton, Animas Forks, and Red Mountain, was constructed with boards stacked flat for stoutness. The jail is located in the town park east of downtown Telluride.

Visitors to the Tomboy Mine today find it hard to imagine the size of the mining and milling operation at the site during the late 1890s. (Courtesy of the Colorado Historical Society, negative F-6007.)

The crumbling remnants of the Smuggler-Union tram house stand near the ruins of Tomboy. The tram sent ore all the way down to the Smuggler-Union (now the Pandora) Mill, about three thousand feet below.

The Telluride Historical Museum, housed in the 1895 hospital, is located one block north on Gregory, near the beginning of Tomboy Road. It was closed for renovation when I visited in 1997, but I had enjoyed touring it several years before.

Southwest of the business district at the end of Townsend is the renovated Rio Grande Southern Depot, now a restaurant.

Five blocks east of the depot on Pacific, between Pine and Spruce, stand two brothels, the Senate and the Silverbell; two cribs; and a madam's residence—vestiges of Telluride's notorious red light district. Around the corner from the bordellos is a stone jail attached to the public library.

The turnoff to Lone Tree Cemetery is beyond the park on the way to Pandora. There you will find graves of Finns, Swedes, Italians, Austrians, Greeks, and others. Located near the flagpole is the largest monument, a reminder of the labor troubles that plagued area mines in the early 1900s. It was erected by the 16 to 1 Miners' Union in memory of Finland's John Barthell, who died at the Smuggler on July 3, 1901 (two months after the beginning of a bitter and violent strike). His epitaph resonates like an union's call to arms:

In the world's broad field of battle,
In the bivouac of life
Be not like dumb driven cattle
Be a hero in the strife.

Pandora

Driving east from Lone Tree Cemetery, you will pass the townsite of Liberty Bell with its mill remnants and a series of red-roofed white buildings. A mile beyond is the entrance to the immense Smuggler-Union (Pandora) Mill.

Originally called Newport after a town in Kentucky when it was settled in 1876, the town became Pandora in 1881 because the Pandora Mining Company was the major employer. The mill town was in a spectacularly steep canyon, resulting in practically annual snowslides. In one avalanche, the first floor of a home was destroyed, killing two women. But the second floor dropped so gently that a child on that floor was virtually unhurt. When the Rio Grande Southern extended tracks to Pandora, much of route was encased in heavy-duty snowsheds.

Some of Pandora was covered by giant tailings piles west of the mill. A reclamation project began on those tailings in 1992, forcing Pandora's last residents to vacate.

A trail to Bridal Veil Falls (at 365 feet, the longest freefall in Colorado) begins .3 of a mile past the mill. At the top of the falls stands a restored 1904 hydroelectric plant that operated until 1954. It can still generate five hundred kilowatts of power daily.

The Tomboy Mine

Go to the Tomboy Mine not because of its remains—most of it is mere debris—but because you reach it by one of the most spectacular, scenic drives in the San Juans. To travel to the Tomboy Mine from Telluride, go north on Oak to Tomboy Road, a narrow, one-lane route frequently crowded during tourist season. You don't need four-wheel drive, but I certainly recommend a high-clearance vehicle and an experienced mountain-road driver (or take a commercial back-roads tour).

Located only five miles from Telluride but a stunning three thousand feet above it in Savage Basin, the Tomboy was one of the richest gold mines in the district. The Tomboy claim was filed in 1880, but it wasn't until 1894 that large-scale operations began, eventually financed by Shanghai and London investors. The community featured the requisite mining buildings, a store, a stable, and a school, along with such niceties as tennis courts, a bowling alley, and reportedly the highest YMCA in the United States. A daily stage provided passenger and mail service between Tomboy and Telluride.

When you arrive at Tomboy, the first thing you will notice, in addition to the gorgeous views, is that rubble is everywhere; virtually every flat spot has foundations, slabs of concrete, fragments of metal, or broken bricks.

The largest ruins are the stamp mill foundations. Much of the supporting structure was made of timbers, because only wood could withstand the vibrations of the crashing stamps at the freezing temperatures in which the mill often operated. Attached to one side of the mill was a two-hole outhouse that simply had a vertical drop below it. A former mill worker said that in winter, snow would blow up through the outhouse seats, creating an "invigorating" experience.

Nearby rock pillars were part of a three-story boarding house. The remnants of its vault remain amid the pillars.

On a hill above the boarding house ruins is a large tin-covered wood building, which reportedly was the mine company office or the company's guest quarters. Incidentally, the road deteriorates noticeably beyond Tomboy as it ascends Imogene Pass and heads down to Ouray.

When You Go

Telluride is 11 miles northeast of Ophir Loop on State Route 145. Pandora is 2 miles east of Telluride; the Tomboy Mine is 5 miles east of Telluride. See text for specific directions.

Dreams of gold and silver brought people to mountains a century ago, but it is the dramatic scenery and echoes of the past that draw them today.

Glossary of Mining Terms

adit: A nearly horizontal entrance to a mine.

arrastra: An apparatus used to grind ore by means of a heavy stone that is dragged around in a circle, normally by mules or oxen.

assay: To determine the value of a sample of ore, in ounces per ton, by using a chemical evaluation.

charcoal kiln (or oven): A structure into which wood is placed and subjected to intense heat through a controlled, slow burning. Charcoal is a longer-lasting, more efficient wood fuel often used to power mills and smelters. If the kiln is used to convert coal to coke, it is a "coke oven."

chloride: Usually refers to ores containing chloride of silver.

claim: A tract of land with defined boundaries that includes mineral rights extending downward from the surface.

diggings: Evidence of mining efforts, such as placer workings.

dredge: An apparatus, usually on a flat-bottomed boat, that scoops material out of a river to extract gold-bearing sand or gravel.

galena: The most common lead mineral.

grubstake: An advance of money, food, and/or supplies to a prospector in return for a share of any discoveries.

headframe: The vertical apparatus over a mine shaft that has cables to be lowered down the shaft for raising either ore or a cage; sometimes called a "gallows frame."

high-grading: The theft of rich ore, usually by a miner working for someone else who owns the mine.

hydraulic mining: A method of mining using powerful jets of water to wash away a bank of gold-bearing earth.

ingot: A cast bar or block of a metal.

lode: A continuous mineral-bearing deposit or vein.

mill: A building in which rock is crushed to extricate minerals by one of several methods. If this is done by stamps (heavy hammers or pestles), it is a stamp mill. If by iron balls, it is a ball mill. The mill is usually constructed on the side of a hill to utilize its slope—hence the term "gravity-fed mill."

mining district: An area of land described (usually for legal purposes) and designated as containing valuable minerals in paying amounts.

Holy Cross City is one of Colorado's hardest-to-reach ghost towns.

Mother Lode: The principal lode passing through a district or section of the country.

mucker: A person or machine that clears material such as rock in a mine.

nugget: A lump of native gold or other mineral.

ore: A mineral of sufficient concentration, quantity, and value to be mined at a profit.

ore-sorting house: A building usually near a mine in which higher-grade ore is sorted from lower-grade ore or waste before being sent to a mill or smelter.

pan: To look for gold by washing earth, gravel, or sand, usually in a stream bed.

placer: A waterborne deposit of sand or gravel containing heavier materials such as gold, which have been eroded from their original bedrock and concentrated as small particles that can be washed, or "panned," out.

prospect: Mineral workings of unproven value.

salting: To place valuable minerals in a place in which they do not really occur. Done to deceive.

shaft: A vertical or nearly vertical opening into the earth for mining.

slag: The waste product of a smelter; hence, slag dumps.

smelter: A building or complex in which material is melted in order to separate impurities from pure metal.

tailings: Waste or refuse left after milling is complete; sometimes used more generally, although incorrectly, to indicate waste dumps.

tellurium: A rare element usually combined with metals, as with gold and silver in sylvanite.

tramway: An apparatus for moving materials such as ore, rock, or even supplies in buckets suspended from pulleys that run on a cable.

waste dump: Waste rock that comes out of the mine but which is not of sufficient value to warrant milling; usually found immediately outside the mine entrance.

workings: A general term indicating any mining development.

wye: A railroad track in the shape of a "Y" (except that track is across the top of the Y) that enables a train to reverse direction.

Bibliography

Aldrich, John K. *Ghosts of Clear Creek County.* Lakewood, Colorado: Centennial Graphics, 1984 (rev. 1992).

———. *Ghosts of Gilpin County.* Lakewood, Colorado: Centennial Graphics, 1985 (rev. 1996).

———. *Ghosts of Summit County.* Lakewood, Colorado: Centennial Graphics, 1986 (rev. 1992).

———. *Ghosts of the Western San Juans,* vol 1. Lakewood, Colorado: Centennial Graphics, 1988 (rev. 1991).

Arizona Daily Star, 8 January 1995.

Ashcroft Journal, 2 May 1882.

Bancroft, Caroline. *Augusta Tabor: Her Side of the Scandal.* Boulder, Colorado: Johnson Books, 1955 (sixth edition, 1970).

———. *Unique Ghost Towns and Mountain Spots.* Boulder, Colorado: Johnson Books, 1961.

Benson, Maxine. *1001 Colorado Place Names.* Lawrence, Kansas: University Press of Kansas, 1994.

Dallas, Sandra. *Colorado Ghost Towns and Mining Camps.* Norman, Oklahoma: University of Oklahoma Press, 1985.

Denver Post, 12 November 1995.

Ellis, Anne. *The Life of an Ordinary Woman.* New York: Houghton Mifflin Company, 1929. Reprinted Boston: Houghton Mifflin Company, 1990.

Empire Magazine, 23 July 1978.

Feitz, Leland. *Ghost Towns of the Cripple Creek District.* Colorado Springs: Little London Press, 1974.

Granruth, Alan. *A Guide to Downtown Central City, Colorado.* Black Hawk, Colorado: One Stop Printing and Graphics, 1989 (rev. 1991).

Levine, Brian. *Cripple Creek: City of Influence.* Cripple Creek: Historic Preservation Department, City of Cripple Creek, 1994.

Mead, Jay (Editor). *Silver Plume Walking Tour.* People for Silver Plume, n.d.

Moynihan, Betty. *Augusta Tabor, A Pioneering Woman.* Evergreen, Colorado: Cordillera Press, 1988.

Neely, Cynthia; Walter R. Borneman; Christine Bradley. *Guide to the Georgetown-Silver Plume Historic District.* Boulder, Colorado: Johnson Printing, 1995.

Noel, Thomas J.; Paul F. Mahoney; Richard E. Stevens. *Historical Atlas of Colorado.* Norman and London: University of Oklahoma Press, 1994.

Osterwald, Doris B. *Cinders and Smoke.* Lakewood, Colorado: Western Guideways, Ltd., 1965 (sixth edition, 1989).

Rhine, Stanley. *Galloping Geese on the Rio Grande Southern.* Golden, Colorado: Colorado Railroad Museum, 1971.

Rocky Mountain News, 8 July 1997; 15 July 1997.

Rowe, Jim and Louise. *Portal into the Past.* Granite, Colorado: Clear Creek Canyon Historical Society of Chaffee County, Inc., n.d.

San Juan Courier (A Periodical Publication of the San Juan Historical Society), Summer 1997.

Stoehr, C. Eric. *Bonanza Victorian.* Albuquerque: University of New Mexico Press, 1975.

Ubbelohde, Carl; Maxine Benson; Duane A. Smith. *A Colorado History* (seventh edition). Boulder Colorado: Pruett Publishing Company, 1995.

Varney, Philip. *Arizona Ghost Towns and Mining Camps.* Phoenix: Arizona Highways Publications, 1994.

Weis, Norman D. *Helldorados, Ghosts and Camps of the Old Southwest.* Caldwell, Idaho: The Caxton Printers, Ltd., 1977.

Wolle, Muriel Sibell. *The Bonanza Trail.* Chicago: Swallow Press, 1953.

———. *Stampede to Timberline.* Chicago: Swallow Press, 1949 (rev. 1974).

Acknowledgments

Philip Varney

For assistance in historical research: Alpine Tunnel Historical Association and volunteer Tom Clauter; Arizona Historical Society and Kim Frontz, Karen Greenberg, and Mary Flynn; Aspen Historical Society and Mary Beth Pepper, assistant director; Clear Creek Canyon Historical Society of Chaffee County; Colorado Historical Society Library and Barbara Dey and Rebecca Lintz; Denver Public Library Western History Department; Durango & Silverton Narrow Gauge Railroad and Kristi Nelson; Gilpin County Historical Society and James J. Prochaska, executive director; Marble Historical Society and Joseph Manz, president; San Juan County Historical Society and Beverly Rich, chairman; the Hotel de Paris and Velma Ferguson; Historic Georgetown, Inc. and Ronald J. Neely, president; the Wheeler Opera House and Nida A. Tautvydas, executive director, and Christine Hipp, house manager; Tommi Holden of Fun Time Jeep Tours in Salida; and Greg Kazel, Como Roundhouse Preservation, Inc.

For field-work support: Suzanne Lawder, Darrell and Joyce Oldridge, Janet Varney, Jim Janoviak and Karen Daly, Nick Alsever, Mike Moore, Joan Euler, John and Susan Drew, Maegan Williams and Kristen Yarber, Marc and Kristy Psaltis, Matt Psaltis, Greg Psaltis and family, Dennis Judstra, Fred and Milly Hardie, Betty Rowe, Nancy Reed, John and Roberta Crawford.

For historical photographs: The Aspen Historical Society, the Colorado Historical Society, the Denver Public Library, Greg Kazel, and Ted Kierscey.

A rare unoccupied home in Cripple Creek shows the skill of a carpenter and his lathe.

For their efforts in preserving Colorado's historic places: the Colorado Historical Society, the Ghost Town Club of Colorado, and the San Juan Advocates.

For his diligence in keeping Colorado history alive through his newspaper columns, books, and lectures: Tom Noel.

For photography: John Drew. In this, my sixth book, I have for the first time completely given over the photography to someone else. I especially wish to acknowledge John and his wife Susan, who have assisted me in ways I have no space to explain. It is highly likely that you picked up this book based on his images, not my text.

John Drew

I would particularly like to acknowledge Arthur Tremayne of Cripple Creek, Curt Claus and Lisa Worley at the Hotel de Paris in Georgetown, and Kristi Nelson at the Durango & Silverton Narrow Gauge Railroad. Editor Amy Rost-Holtz at Voyageur Press is a pleasure to work with and has provided gentle nudges on several occasions.

Working with a writer such as Philip Varney is a delight; he has been skillful and resourceful and has made my job much easier by providing information about the sites ahead of time. Philip is a talented photographer in his own right and has been able to suggest photographic opportunities that have made the book more visually exciting.

My wife and helpmate Susan has given me companionship and encouragement throughout this book. She is also a professional photographer and has been a tremendous resource.

Index

159

About the Photographer and Author

John Drew and Philip Varney (Photo by Susan Gibler Drew)

John Drew

Photographer John Drew's images have been featured in *Arizona Highways* magazine, as well as many calendars, books, and catalogs. His photographic work has taken him throughout the western United States and around the globe to locations such as Kenya, Czechoslovakia, and Thailand. He also teaches workshops and seminars in photography throughout the western United States.

A former dentist, he left that profession and became a photographer at the age of forty-eight. In addition to his skill with a camera, he is an accomplished chef, fly fisherman, and landscape gardener.

He currently lives in Wyoming with his wife, photographer Susan Gibler Drew.

Philip Varney

Philip Varney was in high school when his family moved from Illinois to Arizona. He quickly became fascinated by the history of the West, especially when finding that history meant exploring scenic back roads. Today, he travels extensively, both by car and bicycle, in the western United States.

Ghost Towns of Colorado is his fifth book on ghost towns. In his previous books, he took readers to visit the ghost towns of Arizona, New Mexico, and Southern California. He is also the author of a book on bicycle tours in southern Arizona and is a regular contributor to *Arizona Highways* magazine. His next book for Voyageur Press will be on the ghost towns of Northern California.

He currently makes his home in Tucson.